ORAL INTERPRETATION & THE TEACHING OF ENGLISH

A Collection of Readings

*Edited by Thomas L. Fernandez, Emory University, Atlanta, Georgia
formerly of Monmouth College, Monmouth, Illinois*

A publication of the Illinois State-Wide Curriculum Study Center in the Preparation of Secondary School English Teachers (ISCPET)

NATIONAL COUNCIL OF TEACHERS OF ENGLISH

NCTE Committee on Publications

Robert F. Hogan, NCTE Executive Secretary, *Chairman*
Charlotte S. Huck, Ohio State University
Henry W. Sams, Pennsylvania State University
Mildred E. Webster, St. Joseph Senior High School, St. Joseph, Michigan
Enid M. Olson, NCTE Director of Publications, 1960-69
Eugene C. Ross, NCTE Director of Publications, 1969-

Consultant Readers

Rae Dodge, Wilson High School, Portland, Oregon
Edward J. Pappas, Wayne State University

Book Design

Norma Phillips, NCTE Headquarters

Library of Congress Catalog Card Number 75-91828
NCTE Stock Number 26965
Second Printing 1975

Copyright © 1969
National Council of Teachers of English
1111 Kenyon Road, Urbana, Illinois 61801
Printed in the United States of America

ACKNOWLEDGMENT

To the credit of the academic profession, we occasionally produce men who are in each sense of the word teacher. They are uniquely capable of *doing* themselves what they inspire others to do. Nick Hook is such a man.

Monmouth, Illinois　　　　　　　　　　　　　　　　　　　　T. L. F.
May 29, 1969

CONTENTS

Foreword	vii
Robert F. Hogan, National Council of Teachers of English	
Permissions	ix
The Act of Literature and the Act of Interpretation	1
Wallace A. Bacon, Northwestern University	
Oral Interpretation as an Approach to Literature	9
Frances L. McCurdy, University of Missouri	
Oral Interpretation as an Aid to the Understanding of Literature	17
Margaret M. Neville, DePaul University	
Oral Interpretation: An Extension of Literary Study	21
Allen Bales, University of Alabama	
Teaching Delivery Techniques of Oral Interpretation	29
Willard J. Friederich, Marietta College	
A Supervisor Looks at the Teaching of Literature in the High School	37
Clarence W. Hach, Evanston Township High School	
Readers Theatre and the Short Story	45
Elizabeth Worrell, Northeast Missouri State College	
Why Read to High School Students?	53
Vernell G. Doyle, Arlington Heights High School	
Uses of Oral Interpretation in Directing and Motivating the Outside Reading of High School Students	59
Dorothy Matthews, University of Illinois	
Findings and Recommendations of the ISCPET Conference on Oral Interpretation	71
T. L. Fernandez	
Appendix I: ISCPET Staff	83
Appendix II: Background of the ISCPET Conference	85
Appendix III: Report of the Study	88
Appendix IV: ISCPET Oral Interpretation Survey	93
Appendix V: Bibliography	95

FOREWORD

Approaches to the teaching of literature in the secondary school are almost bewildering in their variety. Too often, however, an individual teacher swears by one approach—*his* approach—by which he means the approach that dominated his study of literature as an undergraduate. Or the approach he adopted after rejecting that one. For one person, this means historical development in genres or literary forms. For another, it means close study and explication of the lonely text. For yet another, the approach is by topic or theme. But even if final choices are sometimes too narrow, at least the range of possible choices is substantial.

Yet for all the available approaches, none is more ignored than oral interpretation. This is not to say that elementary teachers do not read stories and poems to primary children on rainy days, or that some high school classes do not occasionally or even regularly read *Macbeth* aloud. But reading aloud and bringing both insight and discipline to oral interpretation are vastly different matters.

The reasons for the low frequency of oral interpretation are complex. Part of the problem, surely, is in the departmental divisions of those colleges and universities that prepare most of the teachers. Part, too, probably stems from the existence of separate professional societies for teachers of English, of speech, and of drama. Some credit must surely go to the strong position that the "new criticism" has enjoyed in the undergraduate literature curriculum. Also involved are certification practices and requirements. According to a survey undertaken by NCTE in 1963, fewer than 5 percent of secondary school English teachers nationally reported a major in speech, drama, or theater; another 8 percent reported completing a minor in any of these fields. Such percentages are hardly enough to shift the center of gravity in the English teaching profession at large.

The papers that follow were originally prepared for and delivered at a conference on oral interpretation sponsored by the Illinois State-Wide Curriculum Study Center in the Preparation of Secondary School English Teachers (ISCPET) at Monmouth College, Monmouth, Illinois, June 24-28, 1968. Although the conference itself was necessarily concerned with the preparation of teachers in Illinois, the range of issues raised by the speakers is far broader. It is in fact national.

Consequently, the National Council of Teachers of English was delighted to have an opportunity to consider for publication the conference papers as a collection of readings for teachers of English and for those who prepare English teachers. It was the unanimous recommendation of independent readers and the Committee on Publications that the Council take advantage of the opportunity. To appeal to a much larger audience—members of the Council and other English teachers across the country—we have reordered parts of the report that was originally prepared for the participating institutions involved in the ISCPET project. The Council's "edition" begins forthrightly with the substantive papers that served as position statements for the ISCPET conference.

But to keep them as matters of permanent record, the background material on the conference and the report of the study by Mr. Fernandez which preceded the conference appear in appendices. We are confident that secondary school teachers of English and English educators across the country will find the papers here collected interesting and instructive. Professional leaders in other states, should they wish to undertake status studies of teacher preparation in oral interpretation to be followed up by similar conferences, will find considerable help in the appendices.

Robert F. Hogan

PERMISSIONS

The editor, authors, and publishers express appreciation to the following agencies and firms for permission to cite illustrative passages of poetry and fiction:

Chatto & Windus Ltd., London, England, and the Literary Estate of William Faulkner, for the passages from "Was" from GO DOWN, MOSES by William Faulkner.

Faber and Faber Ltd., London, England, for the lines from "O, What Is That Sound?" from COLLECTED SHORTER POEMS 1927-1957, by W. H. Auden, published by Faber and Faber Ltd.

Holt, Rinehart and Winston, Inc., New York, for the lines from "Two Tramps in Mud Time" from COMPLETE POEMS OF ROBERT FROST. Copyright© 1964 by Lesley Frost Ballantine. Reprinted by permission of Holt, Rinehart and Winston, Inc.

Alfred A. Knopf, Inc., New York, for the lines from "Piazza Piece." Copyright 1927 by Alfred A Knopf, Inc., and renewed 1955 by John Crowe Ransom. Reprinted from SELECTED POEMS, Revised Edition, by John Crowe Ransom, by permission of the publisher.

MacGibbon & Kee Ltd., London, England, for "This Is Just to Say" from William Carlos Williams, COLLECTED EARLIER POEMS, by permission of MacGibbon & Kee Ltd.

The Macmillan Company, New York, for the Lines from "September, 1913" from COLLECTED POEMS by William Butler Yeats. Copyright 1916 by The Macmillan Company, renewed 1944 by Bertha Georgie Yeats. Reprinted with permission of The Macmillan Company.

New Directions Publishing Corporation, New York, for "This Is Just to Say" from William Carlos Williams, COLLECTED EARLIER POEMS. Reprinted by permission of New Directions Publishing Corporation.

Laurence Pollinger Limited, London, England, for the lines from "Two Tramps in Mud Time" from THE COMPLETE POEMS OF ROBERT FROST, published by Jonathan Cape Limited; and

for the lines from "Piazza Piece" from SELECTED POEMS by John Crowe Ransom, published by Eyre & Spottiswood Ltd.

Random House, Inc., New York, for the lines from "O, What Is That Sound?" Copyright 1937 and renewed 1965 by W. H. Auden. Reprinted from COLLECTED SHORTER POEMS 1927-1957, by W. H. Auden, by permission of Random House, Inc.; and

for the passages from "Was." Copyright 1942 by William Faulkner. Reprinted from GO DOWN, MOSES by William Faulkner, by permission of Random House, Inc.

A. P. Watt & Son, London, England, for the lines from "September, 1913" from COLLECTED POEMS OF W. B. YEATS, by permission of Mr. M. B. Yeats and the Macmillan Companies of Canada & London.

The Act of Literature and the Act of Interpretation ✺ Wallace A. Bacon

The context in which I am discussing both literature and interpretation is the context with which teachers of English and speech are particularly concerned—literature and interpretation thought of as serving the needs of students and of teachers on the secondary school level. Let me begin by setting down my key words. They are *act, feeling, communion, event,* and *embodiment*. All are concerned with movement. All are tensive. All involve process and becoming.

Literature in the classroom has served a variety of purposes. Susanne Langer has pointed out that although we regularly expect students to devote themselves to the study of English, we wouldn't think of making equal demands for painting or music or sculpture or dance. That is because much of the teaching of English has very little to do with literature as literature.[1] It becomes an interest in spelling, grammar, vocabulary building, exposition, biography, history, sociology, psychology, philosophy, and so on. My concern is with literature as literature—with literature as an art form. If I were to single out the primary objective in the teaching of both literature and interpretation it would be, for me, simply this: to lead students to the experiencing of literature as a felt form. What I value above all is that moment when, as Wallace Stevens puts it in one of his poems, "The reader becomes the book...."[2] This impact of the poem as a felt form is what the poet and the poem and the reader have always valued most about literature, though teachers and critics often find it (as Archibald MacLeish has put it) easier to talk about difficulties in poetry than to talk about poetry itself.[3]

One of the essays in a recent publication by the Illinois State-Wide Curriculum Study Center in the Preparation of Secondary

School English Teachers presumably devotes itself to the concern which I am here expressing.[4] But the essay tips its hand when it says (as if the issue were clear and unquestionable) that surely it is more important for the student to know the impact of paradox than to know the difference between an iambus and a trochee. The relationship of meter and rhythm to total form is of so basic and pervasive a nature that I am forced finally to say that this writer and I must mean very different things by the phrase "literature as literature." If literary study, whatever else it may do for the student, sends him away from, or never brings him to, that response which Stevens describes, when book and reader are one, then literary study has failed him. The language of literature is symbolism with an immediate rather than a mediate purpose. It wants not to be paraphrased, nor applied, but to be felt.[5] What most poems want (they are like us) is to be loved for themselves.

As Susanne Langer has lately been demonstrating in her volume entitled *Mind: An Essay on Human Feeling*, living forms are made up of acts.[6] The act is the basic unit of life forms. It has as its characteristics these stages: inception, acceleration, climax, and cadence or falling off. The act of the poem shares these very characteristics with all other living forms. Literature is made up of acts, larger acts subsuming smaller acts, each work with its own pacemaker rhythm governing smaller rhythms. Poems are thus, in symbolic form (i.e., language), alive. They share property of all living organisms—tensiveness, the state of aliveness which shows itself in stresses and strains between ideas, between pitch levels, between images, between values, between ideas, between various meanings of a single word, between characters in a play, between emotions, between the components of metaphor and simile, and so on. The ways of defining tensiveness are almost infinite.

The formal structure within which these acts occur is the habitat of the poem's life. Form is the habitat of life.[7] The formal arrangement which we call the poem is the external surface which both separates the form from the rest of the world and is the means of contact with it.[8] Until the acts of the poem are felt, they may be said to be unconscious, since consciousness is the felt level of acts.[9]

The reader, in reading, brings—or should bring—the poem to consciousness, so that the feeling symbolized in and through the language of the poem becomes actualized, realized, experienced, though somewhat differently from reader to reader, and probably always imperfectly, since the perfect reader doubtless doesn't exist in this world. The realization of the *act* of a poem is an *event*.

I do not want anything I have said to suggest that I am not interested in "meaning." I am not arguing for emotionalizing. As I use the term, "feeling" involves perception; it is meaning not abstracted, not disembodied, that I value, but meaning embodied in living form.[10] When I talk with students about Act I, Scene 1, of *Julius Caesar*, I am not interested primarily in knowing what a pun is, or what the functions of the tribune were in ancient Rome, or what the Lupercal was, but in knowing what is going on, and what the people are doing, and what the tribunes are feeling, and what happens between all those people on the stage. The so-called "facts" are important enough in their way, but their function is what matters finally. Too often teaching never gets beyond the "facts." The facts which go into the making up of a poem are simply materials. It is not the materials which are to be felt, but the structure into which the materials have gone.[11] What we are after is the sense of presence into which these materials have coalesced.[12] The range and weight of a poem's ideas matter very greatly when we come to evaluate the poem; but in defining poem as poem, it is not the range and weight of the ideas but the symbolic *act* with which we are first and foremost concerned. If one asks a high school student what Ariel's song in *The Tempest* means—"Full fathom five thy father lies . . ."—he will not get very far with the student's answer, providing that he gets any answer at all. What the poem *means* is what the poem *is*. It is definable more as event, as quality, than as idea.

The poem—to recapitulate—is an act, an event. When realized, it is a felt event. Of course it is man-made, and our problem is complicated by the fact that it exists in language, which we ordinarily think of as an instrument of communication. Man usually uses language discursively. Poems do—and must—communicate if we are to feel or value them. But I think it a mistake to think of a poem as communication, or as persuasion, or even by any necessity as discourse. There are poems where I think it very unhelpful to think of the presence of a *speaker* of the poem.[13] Rhetoric (the art of persuasion by devices of language) is a tool used often by the poet, but it is not the poem itself. The sense of a speaker is a tool used often by the poet, but it is not the poem itself. It is not the function of a poem (except for those pieces we speak of separately as propaganda or thesis pieces) to communicate to me—any more than it is the function of a carrot or of a sunset or of a bull moose to communicate to me. Poems exist. Like all living forms, they grow, they falter, they change, they may die. We can hurt them, or kill them off, individually. We can and should commune with them, join together in the celebration of life. I can communicate with you *about* a poem. I don't think it is my function as reader or interpreter to communicate *via* a poem, though it may be my function as a speaker or even, at times, as a teacher. But the teacher who always uses a poem is not serving the poem as poem. I find it humiliating, as an interpreter, to be told that the interpreter's task is to tell or show an audience something which he already knows and which he is about to pass along to them. I should argue instead that what the interpreter does is rather to actualize the poem, to make it in his own person audible and visible as a felt experience. He does communicate, but this is a result of what he centrally does, and not the heart of it. The poem alive is what is central—the poem alive, which is to say the poem as presence, with a perspective, with its own tensions, its coalescent form. The interpreter, in the most literal sense, *embodies* the poem.

Let me go all the way down this road, which will seem to you to have led me into the vast darknesses. I have been suggesting that interpretation is active. The interpreter performs—and let me urge you to think of this as a good, healthy, creditable activity, not to be confused with exhibitionism or self-service. All life performs. I should like to argue now that the silent reader, too, must perform if he is to experience literature. It is not only the oral reader who embodies. The silent reader must embody.[14] And the fact of the matter is that the failure of silent reading of literature often resides simply here—that silent readers are not taught how to perform. They are asked questions, instead—How many people are in this story? Where is Davenport, Iowa? In what famous cemetery was the author buried? What is a mongoose? Where did Desdemona get her handkerchief? What kind of plant was on the windowsill? I don't want to seem simply to laugh at these questions. Indeed, they may be very important in getting to the ultimate concern. But they are not the ultimate concern, and students should not be led to expect that they are.

Let me try quickly to illustrate a little of what I mean by talking about, and reading, a poem by William Carlos Williams called "This Is Just to Say." I always think of it as a written note—something a husband might leave for his wife on the kitchen table. It says, as a note, "I have eaten the plums that were in the icebox, and which you were probably saving for breakfast. Forgive me, they were delicious. So sweet and so cold." That is the note, as a piece of communication. It isn't yet the poem. I can give it a greater degree of formality by interrupting the temporal sequence at fixed moments:

"I have eaten the plums / that were in the icebox, / and which you were probably / saving for breakfast. / Forgive me; they were delicious. / So sweet and so cold." But this isn't yet Williams' poem. The communication is clear—but it was clear the first time. The tensions are not yet adequately defined, for Williams' taste. We give the poem its real form—its real life—by promoting further pauses as an aspect of its prosody. We look more attentively at it as felt form. The humor grows—and so, perhaps, does the affection—as the writer of the note thinks of the reader who will find it. Here is the poem as Williams finally arranges it on the page:

> I have eaten
> the plums
> that were in the icebox
>
> and which
> you were probably
> saving
> for breakfast
>
> Forgive me
> they were delicious
> so sweet
> and so cold.[15]

How little of the poem one would get if, asking a student "What does this poem mean? he were to get the answer, "It means that somebody ate the plums that were being saved for breakfast." Perhaps it is clear, at this point, that giving the poem its life means allowing it to contain within it *all* that it will contain. The best reading of a poem is the most comprehensive reading—though it must be recognized that some readers try to stuff into poems *more* than they can profitably contain. One must always remember the stricture quoted by Auden from C. G. Lichtenberg: "If an ass looks into a book, one cannot expect an apostle to peer out."[16]

If we admit, then, the possibility that a poem may be thought of as an act, as a presence (and not necessarily as a human presence), we shall find it easier to agree that poems *are*, and that we are meant to feel them and all the weight and width of the acts they enclose. And if we are successful as readers (whether silent or oral), and if they are successful as poems (or even if we or they are only partly successful), we do feel them. What we have is not communication—someone telling us something—but communion, a sharing of something which we and the poem hold in common. It is the communality of what is that is valuable to us. But this communality is something created in the exchange between the poem and us, not simply something which we bring to the poem. The poem is indeed, at the moment of its being experienced, the act of the mind experiencing it, the body embodying it. The act is a conscious act—that is, it is a felt act. It is an event. The form of the act is determined in part by the living form of the poem—a symbolic expression of feeling—and partly by the living form of the reader. The poetic experience, looked at this way, is the poem incarnate.

Notes

1. Susanne K. Langer, *Feeling and Form* (New York: Charles Scribner's Sons, 1953), p. 208.
2. In "The House Was Quiet and the World Was Calm."
3. Granville Hicks, in a review of Wright Morris, *A Bill of Rites, a Bill of Wrongs, a Bill of Goods* (New York: New American Library, 1968), quotes Morris and refers to MacLeish: " 'The idea that books are safes with secret combinations, and poems are ingenious double crostics, is not new, but only recently has achieved the status of a doctrine.' The doctrine is a boon to professors, who, as Archibald MacLeish put it, find it easier to teach difficulties than poetry. 'What *study* does to what used to be reading' is a disaster, Morris says." One may share part of Morris' indignation without going all the way down his path. The heart and the imagination do get short shrift in many classrooms. Hicks' review is in *Saturday Review*, March 16, 1968, pp. 29-30.
4. John S. Gerrietts, "What Literature—and Why?" in *Issues in the Preparation of Teachers of English*, ed. Raymond D. Crisp (Urbana: University of Illinois Press, November 1967), pp. 19-24. This is a publication of the Illinois State-Wide Curriculum Study Center in the Preparation of Secondary School English Teachers (ISCPET). Mr. Gerrietts' essay raises a number of debatable issues.
5. I would say, as I have said elsewhere, that they are not simply to be "understood"—but the word "understood" has given trouble to some readers who have taken it erroneously to indicate that I am not concerned with meaning.
6. It will be clear enough to readers of Mrs. Langer's book that I am very much indebted to it—and that it has given me a great deal of trouble, though she is not to be blamed for my particular applications of her arguments. The complete reference is Susanne K. Langer, *Mind: An Essay on Human Feeling*, Vol. I (Baltimore: The Johns Hopkins Press, 1967).
7. The notion that form is the habitat of life comes specifically from Gaston Bachelard, *The Poetics of Space* (New York: Grossman Publishers, Inc., 1964), p. 114.
8. An idea from Langer, *Mind*, p. 421. But she is speaking of life forms rather than of art forms.
9. *Ibid.*, p. 438.
10. This is the sense of the word *feeling* in such a question as "How do you feel about the United Nations?" where we expect the answer to give us total response—attitudes, ideas, uncertainties, questions; and the more seriously we ask the question, the more finely articulated we expect the answer to be. This is not quite the same as the sense involved when we say "How do

you feel?" In the latter case, we seem to be asking more simply about a "physical" or an emotional condition, though surely we do not limit the question to that.

11. The terms *materials* and *structure* are used as in René Wellek and Austin Warren, *Theory of Literature* (3rd ed.; New York: Harcourt, Brace & World Inc., 1956), p. 19.

12. *Presence* as a term is from Philip Wheelwright, *Metaphor and Reality* (Bloomington: Indiana University Press, 1962). Wheelwright's whole discussion is of the greatest value with respect to the life of literary language.

13. The seminal discussion of the speaker in the poem is doubtless Cleanth Brooks and Robert Penn Warren, *Understanding Poetry* (3rd ed.; New York: Harcourt, Brace & World, Inc., 1960). For the most recent discussion of the matter in interpretation theory, see Don Geiger, *The Dramatic Impulse in Modern Poetics* (Baton Rouge: Louisiana State University Press, 1967). Mr. Geiger's position is one he has argued very effectively here and elsewhere, but I must confess to some misgivings about it as a description of essence. On the question of rhetoric and literature, see Wayne C. Booth, "The Revival of Rhetoric," *PMLA*, LXXX (1965), 8-12. Thomas O. Sloan has written on the values of rhetorical analysis in "Restoration of Rhetoric to Literary Study," *The Speech Teacher*, XVI (March 1967), 91-97. See also his essay "Oral Interpretation—An Overview: Philosophy, Objectives, Content" in *The Communicative Arts and Sciences of Speech*, ed. Keith Brooks (Columbus, O.: Charles E. Merrill Books, Inc., 1967), pp. 270-276, to which I take particular exception in some respects, and Keith Brooks' essay, "The Communicative Act of Oral Interpretation" in the same volume, pp. 297-315. Other volumes reflecting one or another of my areas of concern are Paul N. Campbell, *The Speaking and the Speakers of Literature* (Belmont, Calif.: Dickenson Publishing Company, 1967); Paul Hunsinger, *Communicative Interpretation* (Dubuque, Ia.: William C. Brown Company, Publishers, 1967); Keith Brooks, Eugene Bahn, LaMont Okey, *The Communicative Act of Oral Interpretation* (Boston: Allyn & Bacon, Inc., 1967). I do not at all mean to suggest a quarrel with the whole, or even the large part, of all these studies.

14. Louise Rosenblatt made this same point with respect to silent reading as a performance, in a speech to the Third Annual Suburban League-Northwestern University English Conference in Evanston, Illinois, on May 4, 1968.

15. William Carlos Williams, "This Is Just to Say," in COLLECTED EARLIER POEMS. Copyright 1938 by William Carlos Williams. Reprinted by permission of New Directions Publishing Corporation, New York, and MacGibbon & Kee Ltd., London, England.

16. W. H. Auden, *The Dyer's Hand* (New York: Random House, Inc., 1962), p. 3.

Oral Interpretation as an Approach to Literature ● Frances L. McCurdy

A recent text in oral interpretation defines that art as a study of literature through the medium of oral performance.[1] Not only do teachers of oral interpretation assume that literature can be studied by oral performance, but many creators of literature assume that their work is to be read aloud. Shakespeare assures the subject of Sonnet 81, "You still shall live (such virtue hath my pen) / Where breath most breathes,—even in the mouths of men." Today, as well as in the time before the printed word became dominant, writers continue to stress sound for understanding the totality of their work. John Holmes says of his own approach to writing a poem, "I want to get one I can read aloud in my own most natural speaking voice."[2]

Moreover, the critics, the most scientific of the humanists, attest to the insights gained by oral reading. David Daiches qualifies, it is true, but says, nonetheless, "There are some who can be brought to enter into the rich vitality of a work more effectively by having it read aloud slowly, with proper phrasing and emphasis, than by the most careful analysis of the structure."[3] R. P. Blackmur, who asserts that literature is made afresh as it is known afresh, explains that "it can be fresh only in performance—that is in reading, seeing, and hearing what is actually in it at this place and this time."[4] Teachers of English in Illinois have also declared their belief in the values of preparation in oral interpretation and need no persuasion.[5]

My purpose is to point out one of the several ways in which oral interpretation contributes to the study of literature. As the interpreter embodies the literature into himself and himself into the literature, he responds with verbal and nonverbal gestures. I shall concentrate on one of the elements of verbal gesture—that of tone. Archibald MacLeish reminds us that "tone is always important in any true poem; it is ignored at the reader's peril."[6] It is possible for the silent reader to ignore tone; the oral interpreter cannot.

I use *tone* to mean manipulation of the voice to express an attitude. Laurence Perrine's illustration is apt. He points out that the statement "I'm going to get married today" may be ecstatic as "(Hooray!) I'm going to get married today!" It may be incredulous as "(I can't believe it.) I'm going to get married today." It may be resigned, "I'm going to get married today," or despairing, "I'm going to get married today."[7]

The oral interpreter may well begin his study with the tone of the writer. (I am using tone as Perrine does to indicate an attitude toward a subject or audience.) Swift's "A Modest Proposal" to sell the year-old children of the Irish poor as an article of food is of course satirical, but the interpreter must make a finer distinction to get the particular kind of satire. Satire often has an element of humor. In this essay, Swift's satire is without humor. It is savage and biting. He obviously considers it futile to get the Irish to act in any reasonable, concerted way and offers his outrageous suggestion without any comic relief.[8] In embodying the tone, the oral interpreter must make these distinctions.

Flaubert in *Madame Bovary* is also ironic, but his irony takes a quite different tone. In *Craft of Fiction*, Percy Lubbock discusses Flaubert's method of placing us so that we see Emma through her eyes yet with an aloofness that keeps us from identifying with her. "A hint of irony is always perceptible," Lubbock says, "and it is enough to prevent us from being lost in her consciousness." Lubbock continues in discussing Flaubert's method, "His valuation of her is only implied; it is in his tone—never in his words, which invariably respect her own estimate of herself, that we see her as a foolish woman."[9]

Lubbock's own tone is the subject of an essay by E. M. Forster. Forster points out that Lubbock extends to his characters in *Roman Pictures* an elaborate charity which causes them to appear in a rather worse light than if no charity was wasted on them at all. "It is the comic atmosphere," Forster says, "but sub-acid, meticulously benign."[10] Voicing this sub-acid, meticulously benign tone is the challenge of the interpreter.

The oral reader must not only determine the writer's attitude; he must be aware of the degree of formality in the tone. Where Whitman's tone is conversational, as an American speaking to Americans, John Crowe Ransom is often formal, almost classic. An excerpt from "Piazza Piece" illustrates:

> I am a gentleman in a dust coat trying
> To make you hear. Your ears are soft and small
> And listen to an old man not at all
> They want the young men's whispering and sighing;
> But see the roses on your trellis dying
> And hear the spectral singing of the moon;
> For I must have my lovely lady soon,
> I am a gentleman in a dust coat trying.[11]

Reading these lines in a conversational informal tone makes them ridiculous.

Generally, the tone of a good writer is distinctive. The voice in his work is often consistent, but the oral reader dare not assume that if he knows the general voice he need not seek the specific tone in a particular story or poem. Yeats' contempt for the lack of conviction among the best of his day is voiced frequently and most notably in the "Second Coming." Where the voice of the "Second Coming" is detached, that of "September, 1913" is savage and personal. In "September, 1913" he speaks directly:

> What need you, being come to sense,
> But fumble in a greasy till
> And add the halfpence to the pence
> And prayer to shivering prayer, until
> You have dried the marrow from the bone?
> For man was born to pray and save; ...[12]

The directness of the voice in "September, 1913" illustrates the importance of the narrator. The oral interpreter must not only be aware of the tone of the writer; he must determine the tone of the narrator whom the writer chooses as his fictional voice. The speaker must not be taken for the writer, even in a lyric poem, where the relationship is most personal. The character of the narrator influences every insight into the work of art that recreating the story in the voice and body can give. For example, a story told by an anonymous storyteller maintains the illusion of objectivity. General degrees of objectivity may be voiced. The narrator may be impartial in his focus and limited to reporting, or the narrator may focus upon a main character through whose presence, actions, and thoughts the reader is made to see and understand the story. While focusing on one main character, the narrator can describe all the characters, actions, and their consequences. On the other hand, the fictional voice may be that of a character who participates to a greater or lesser degree in the story. Subjectivity increases with the narrator's level of involvement in the incidents.

The anonymous narrator stands out of view. He invites the reader to let the story speak for itself. Such a narrator tells the story of Faulkner's *The Bear*.[13] (I speak of the short version of this story copyrighted in 1942 by the Curtis Publishing Company and not of the longer version found in *The Portable Faulkner* or *Go Down, Moses*.) This narrator is primarily concerned with the boy, unnamed in this story, but later given the name of Ike McCaslin. The narrator is omniscient. He knows the boy's past, his thoughts, what he hears and sees. Of the boy's past he tells us, until he was ten, "each November he would watch the wagon containing the dogs and the bedding and food and guns and his cousin McCaslin and Tennie's Jim and Sam Fathers too until Sam moved to the camp to live, depart for the Big Bottom, the big woods." Of what he hears and thinks, he says, "Then he heard the dogs." Or "The gun, the boy thought." But while focusing on the boy, the narrator describes the events taking place and provides the words of Sam Fathers and the boy's own father. He lets us know who is speaking by adding "Sam said" or "said his father." Further, this narrator states the center of meaning: there was "a boy who wished to learn humility and pride in order to become skillful and worthy in the woods but found himself becoming so skillful so fast that he feared he would never become worthy because he had not learned humility and pride, although he had tried, until one day an old man who could not have defined either had led him as though by the hand to where an old bear and a little mongrel of a dog showed him that, by possessing one thing other, he would possess them both...."[14] The story's being told by the narrator rather than by the boy himself provides a detachment. We can feel the intensity of the boy but remain cool enough to observe it. The oral reading tests the ability to maintain this tension and detachment. (Faulkner makes many changes in the longer version of this story appearing in *Go Down, Moses*, but he does not change the position of the narrator.)

The oral interpreter deals with a different kind of narrator in Henry James' *The Real Thing*.[15] Here, the narrator is the major character of the story. He is, you remember, an illustrator who tells us of his experience with the Monarchs, a lady and gentleman who wish to pose for him, and with Oronte and Miss Chum, a manservant and a professional model. The narrator's firsthand knowledge gives his eyewitness report credibility but invites the reader to question the depth of his perception. The reader must determine what kind of man is speaking. He judges the narrator not only by what he says but also by his language, his attitudes, his point of view, and his vocabulary. For example, the vocabulary of the narrator in *The Real Thing* is wide in range. His language is that of an educated man; he observes with some sympathy, however reluctant, the distress of the Monarchs. He is ashamed of the magazines that employ him to illustrate the stories of which he is contemptuous. The oral reader who is to counterfeit the speech of this narrator cannot ignore any of these clues to his nature. The interpreter who is to speak in the narrator's tone must see in this story the illustrator's pretensions, his sensibility and lack of it.

Though the narrators differ in these illustrations, each of them speaks to a general audience. The storyteller tells the story to a living audience; he has no fictional audience to whom he must respond. This distinction has implications for the oral reader. The oral interpreter who speaks for a narrator addressing a fictional listener must be alert to the responses of that imagined listener. For example, the passionate woman in Browning's "The Laboratory" watches the reactions of the maker of potions to her demand for a suitable poison.[16] She speaks in a particular place of fumes and vapors surrounded by vials of bright-colored potions. This speaker is a particular character in a particular place interacting with a fictional character who, though he never speaks, must be definitely established. To be sure, the interpreter does not adopt an Italian accent or sniff the fumes, but he must be able to feel the body tensions of this jealous woman, to see the old chemist stooping over his bench, to hear the soft hissing of the vapors in the laboratory, to be aware of the power that the old man now holds and to calculate the use he may make of this power.

When a story is told by the characters, the interpreter must be aware of each character's attitude toward himself, his particular situation, and others in the scene. He must know the function of a particular speech or scene in the total story. To illustrate, in Auden's "O, What Is That Sound?" the voices must give force to the mounting fear, must give life and distinction to the two characters of the fearful woman and the lover. There is no narrator other than the two characters: the woman who asks,

> O what is that sound which so thrills the ear
> Down in the valley drumming, drumming?

and the man who answers,

> Only the scarlet soldiers, dear,
> The soldiers coming.[17]

Without the necessity of embodying the tones, the kind of thrill mentioned in the first line might be left undetermined. Thrill can be delightful; a thrill can be a tremulous excitement that is pleasant, or it can affect as if by something that pierces, that sends a chill up the spine, that makes the pulse falter and leap. The interpreter must determine which thrill is meant. He must become aware of the mounting terror as the troops pass the doctor's gate, the parson's and the farmer's house, and begin to run toward his own door.

Dependence upon the voice of the characters is greatest in drama or dramatic monologue, where characters alone reveal the totality of their story; but whenever the characters speak in their own voices, the oral reader must bring them to life. The voice of the character is distinct from that of the writer or narrator. Faulkner's voice in *The Bear* is brooding, symbolic. Though sometimes awkward, his is the voice of a poet. The narrator is anonymous and detached; he stays out of the story for the most part. The voices of the characters differ from those of the narrator and each other. Old Sam Fathers, son of a slave woman and a Chickasaw Indian chief, is wise in the way of nature. He belongs to the forest, not to the town. His speech is that of an uneducated man, but it is not without dignity. He speaks to the boy: "I want you to learn how to do when you didn't shoot. It's after the chance for the bear or the deer has done already come and gone that men and dogs get killed." The boy's father belongs to the forest, too, but he also belongs to the town and the world of books. He knows—in the sense of embodying it—Keats' "Ode on a Grecian Urn." His words are simple, but his speech is courtly. For example, after he had closed the book from which he read to his son, he said, "She cannot fade, though thou hast not thy bliss, / For ever wilt thou love, and she be fair!"

" 'He's talking about a girl,' the boy said.

" 'He had to talk about something,' McCaslin said. Then he said, 'He was talking about truth. Truth is one. It doesn't change. It covers all things which touch the heart—honor and pride and pity and justice and courage and love. Do you see now? . . .' "[18]

Just as each person in life is different, so characters are different and speak with different voices. The critical importance of recognizing the pattern of characters is emphasized if one thinks of reading aloud. The oral interpreter is faced with the problem of revealing the total person through his speech, not only his words, but his thoughts and his symbolic actions.

I have repeatedly emphasized awareness as a prerequisite of oral interpretation. Oral reading demands that the reader perceive the voices in the literature. Silent reading does not externalize these elements. Certainly the silent reader may perceive the tone just as the lover of music may hear the tones of a Mahler symphony by looking at the score. The oral reader, however, tests his perception in a way that the silent reader does not. He further provides for his listeners elements of tone, voice, and attitude in the total configuration of the story. Oral interpretation is no guarantee that a poem or story will be approached in its totality, but it does provide a test of the extent of approach.

Notes

1. Wallace Bacon, *The Art of Interpretation* (New York: Holt, Rinehart and Winston, Inc., 1966), p. 6.
2. Paul Engle and Joseph Langland (eds.), *Poets' Choice* (New York: Dell Publishing Company, Inc., 1966), p. 63.
3. David Daiches, *Critical Approaches to Literature* (Englewood Cliffs, N.J.: Prentice-Hall, Inc., 1956), p. 392.
4. R. P. Blackmur, "A Burden for Critics," in *Essays in Modern Literary Criticism*, ed. Ray B. West (New York: Holt, Rinehart and Winston, Inc., 1952), pp. 155-156.
5. Thomas L. Fernandez, "Oral Interpretation and Secondary Teachers of English," *The Speech Teacher*, XVII, 1 (January 1968), 30-33.
6. Archibald MacLeish, *Poetry and Experience* (Baltimore: Penguin Books, 1960), p. 96.
7. Laurence Perrine, *Sound and Sense: An Introduction to Poetry* (2nd ed.; New York: Harcourt, Brace & World, Inc., 1956), p. 135.
8. Jonathan Swift, "A Modest Proposal," in Robert Beloof, *The Performing Voice in Literature* (Boston: Little, Brown and Company, 1966), pp. 398-404.
9. Percy Lubbock, "Madame Bovary," reprinted in *Essays in Modern Literary Criticism*, ed. Ray B. West (New York: Holt, Rinehart and Winston, Inc., 1952), p. 449.
10. E. M. Forster, "Pattern and Rhythm," in *Essays in Modern Literary Criticism*, ed. Ray B. West (New York: Holt, Rinehart and Winston, Inc., 1952), p. 432.
11. Sylvan Barnet, Morton Berman, William Burto, *An Introduction to Literature* (Boston: Little, Brown and Company, 1967, 1963, 1961), pp. 400-401. The eight lines from "Piazza Piece" are Copyright 1927 by Alfred A. Knopf, Inc., and renewed 1955 by John Crowe Ransom. Reprinted from SELECTED POEMS, Revised Edition, by John Crowe Ransom, by permission of the publisher. Also in SELECTED POEMS by John Crowe Ransom, published by Eyre & Spottiswoode, London, and used by permission of Laurence Pollinger Limited.
12. A. G. Stock, "September, 1913," in *W. B. Yeats: His Poetry and Thought* (Cambridge: Cambridge University Press, 1964), p. 169. Six lines from "September, 1913" used by permission of Mr. M. B. Yeats and the Macmillan Companies of Canada & London. Also reprinted with permission

of The Macmillan Company, New York, from COLLECTED POEMS by William Butler Yeats, Copyright 1916 by The Macmillan Company, renewed 1944 by Bertha Georgie Yeats.

13. Barnet, *et al.*, pp. 57-71.
14. *Ibid.*, pp. 68-69.
15. *Ibid.*, pp. 150-171.
16. Wilma Grimes and Alethea Mattingly, *Interpretation: Writer, Reader, Audience* (San Francisco: Wadsworth Publishing Company, Inc., 1961), pp. 32-33.
17. Barnet, *et al.*, pp. 446-447. The four lines from "O, What Is That Sound?" are Copyright 1937 and renewed 1965 by W. H. Auden. Reprinted from COLLECTED SHORTER POEMS 1927-1957, by W. H. Auden, by permission of Random House, Inc., and Faber and Faber Ltd., London.
18. *Ibid.*, p. 68.

Oral Interpretation as an Aid to the Understanding of Literature
Margaret M. Neville

We are inclined to think of literature as the written expression of an artist's or even of a nation's ideas and ideals, and to trace its changes through the printed pages which today preserve the works of the centuries. We tend to forget that much we call literature was once delivered orally by scop or troubadour and only later written down. We may forget that those works which first reached the public in printed form contain elements which can best be transmitted by speech. Language is basically an oral means of communication, and the written or printed word is at best an intermediary between author and reader. Only when the reader is able to *hear* (at least in imagination) the words, phrases, and sentences, or the verses, does he come close to the utterance of the author.

Today we put so much emphasis on rapid reading that we often encourage the student to cover pages as fast as he can. We give courses in rapid reading, sometimes claiming that by such accelerated reading we increase comprehension. It is true that a person may train himself, or be trained, to absorb facts from the printed page more quickly. In a sense he is doing for himself what the *Reader's Digest* does in print. A person satisfied by expert rapid reading is apt to prefer a digest of a novel to the original work. Poetry, he will often have to admit, is simply not for him. We admit there are books that deserve to be read only at breakneck speed, but such reading is not fair to the creative artist who has worked hard to express ideas and images perfectly that he may share with a reader his vision of reality.

There is such a thing as creative reading, whereby the reader enters into a kind of partnership with the writer. He gets on the same wavelength and so is prepared to receive the artist's message. He recreates in his own mind the images transmitted by the writer's words. Since words are primarily oral symbols, however, it would be well for him to hear their sounds. The reader who has learned oral interpretation, therefore, is in a better position to understand many aspects of a piece of literature than one who has not learned the techniques. Imaginative reading, even when done silently, is dependent on the ability to interpret orally. Imaginative teaching of literature is doubly dependent on this ability, for a person cannot transmit to others what he does not possess.

Let us consider just a few instances in the reading of literature where oral interpretation can be a definite aid to understanding. First of all, in poetry, whether there is a major emphasis or idea or an emotional experience in the material being presented, the form has a relationship to music. This music cannot be understood or enjoyed unless it can be *heard* in reality, or at least in imagination. We may teach prosody for traditional meters, or discover how many stresses to the line in nonmetrical forms; but unless we employ oral interpretation, we shall find only basic forms and not the individual music of each work.

For example, we usually say Milton's *Paradise Lost* is in iambic pentameter. Students knowing what an iamb is will singsong the first lines thus:

Of man's/ first dis/obe/dience and/ the fruit
Of that/ forbid/den tree/ whose mor/tal taste
Brought death/ into/ the world/ and all/ our woe.

They will not realize that certain words which seem to be in proper places for iambic stress are relatively unimportant musically and intellectually, whereas some in supposedly unstressed positions have a musical importance. *And* in the first line of *Paradise Lost* illustrates the stressed position used for a conjunction, while *brought* at the beginning of the third line has a total sound far too heavy for the unstressed part of an iamb.

A further study of these few lines will reveal that the reader will have to alter the basic iambic pattern by substituting trochees, spondees, and pyrrhics in certain places if he wishes to bring out the intellectual content in terms of the music. He will realize that the word *first* in line one is important; it was man's *first* disobedience, not his subsequent, that Milton writes about. Also it was *disobedience*, not obedience that caused trouble. In line three he will realize that *death* is an important word as idea and *brought* is strong as music. Hence *brought death* cannot be a normal iamb or trochee. Moreover, he will not want to stress the second syllable of *into* in this third line. Eventually he will achieve a scansion and a reading much more reasonable than his original singsong one:

Of man's/ first dis/obed/ience and/ the fruit

Of that/ forbid/den tree/ whose mor/tal taste

Brought death/ into/ the world/ and all/ our woe.

Here it becomes readily apparent that Milton's careful balancing of the substitute spondee and pyrrhic against one another achieves with the iamb a rhythm that is smooth but not monotonous. Similarly his complete integration of intellectual content and musical form becomes clear.

Sometimes it is not intellectual content but expression of emotion that the poet uses rhythmic variation to achieve. For example, in Wordsworth's sonnet to Milton the music of the altered iambic line points up not so much idea as emotion:

Milton/, thou shouldst/ be liv/ing at/ this hour.

Examples could be multiplied from any reputable poet to illustrate this relationship between idea and music or between emotion and music in poetry. All would point to the importance of being able to read aloud with suitable interpretation, if one is to derive the most in pleasure and understanding from the work of a poet. Once the ability is achieved, the effect will easily be carried over to silent reading wherein one may *hear* by imagination.

Drama is meant to be seen and heard, since it is meant to be acted. Still we do read plays silently at times, and it is only by the use of creative reading which is based on an ability to interpret the lines orally that we get the aesthetic experience we should get from reading a play. This does not mean that we must become finished actors to enjoy reading drama; it means, rather, that we must master the use of the voice to reproduce the intellectual and emotional content of the dialogue at a reader's level.

The reader needs to mentally *hear* and *see* the people in a drama in order to have creative reading. Some training and practice in oral interpretation here will do much more for the understanding of a play than the amateur acting out of a scene that has gone on in many a high school classroom. An awkward playing of Caesar with an old sheet for a toga without an understanding of the lines has not done much for appreciation of Shakespeare.

The same approach to understanding character in a play can be used in studying a piece of fiction. He must learn to hear the characters speak and not be satisfied to merely read their words. Through their conversation, characters reveal themselves and their attitude toward others.

In many pieces of fiction and drama there are elements of atmosphere and mood comparable to the same elements in poetry. The author's choice of words to convey images, often a choice based on the very sound of the words, is intended to produce the desired emotional reaction in the reader. The reader who does not cooperate by imaginative reading fails to attain the pleasure he might have had. He may learn what happens in the story, but he will miss a fascinating aesthetic experience.

For an excellent example of atmosphere and mood created in great part by control of sound in words and rhythm in phrases, we might take a few sentences from Lord Dunsany's "Highwayman," noting the use of liquid consonants and deep vowels to produce the desired effect.

> Tom o' the Roads had ridden his last ride, and was now alone in the night. From where he was a man might see the white, recumbent sheep and the black outline of lonely downs, and the grey line of the farther and lonelier downs beyond them; or in the hollows far below him, out of the pitiless wind, he might see the grey smoke of hamlets arising from black valleys. But all alike was black to the eyes of Tom, and all sounds were silence in his ears; only his soul struggled to slip from the iron chains and to pass southwards into Paradise. And the wind blew and blew.[1]

Here what might have been merely a rather gruesome story of the burial of a highwayman becomes a poetic fantasy quietly touched with deep emotion.

These are but a few indications of the possibilities of oral interpretation as an aid to the understanding of literature. There is no intention of denying the value to a class of the teacher's trained reading of pieces of literature for purposes of enlightenment or entertainment. Our emphasis, however, has been on using oral reading to aid one's own understanding of a literary work—understanding which the prospective teacher must reach before he can transmit knowledge and induce appreciation in a classroom.

Note
1. From Lord Dunsany, *A Dreamer's Tales and Other Stories* (London and New York: G. P. Putnam's Sons, O.P.).

Oral Interpretation: An Extension of Literary Study ❂ Allen Bales

It seems to me that composers and painters have the advantage when it comes to giving a title to their works. They simply pop a number on it: Opus 37 or Study No. 10. When I first started work on this paper, there were many times I wished for just such an advantage, for then I would be free to range all over the fields of oral interpretation and literary study. But that advantage was denied me the moment I elected to call my paper "Oral Interpretation: An Extension of Literary Study." Thus, I limited myself to the extent to which I might range over the fields of our mutual interest. I was bound, in part at least, to show how oral interpretation *is* an extension of literary study.

Now it was not the major terms in the title which caused me some regret. I had little doubt that there would be complete agreement as to the meaning of oral interpretation and literary study. That is not to say that in teaching interpretation there are not differences in emphasis. I, for example, place a great deal of emphasis on the vocal and physical expression of the literature. Some English teachers in the study of literature may place the emphasis on the historical, biographical, and social significance of the work. On the other hand, others may spend little or no time on these aspects. They may prefer instead to dwell on such things as theme, tone, diction, imagery, meter, plot, point of view, etc. Neither was there any doubt in my mind that both interpretation and literary study aimed at making the reader of literature a wiser and more sensitive human being.

What did cause some doubt, if not regret, was that word *extension*. My fears were that oral interpretation might be thought of as something merely *added* to or tacked on to literary study: the way the man in the TV commercial tries to add or tack the filter from one cigarette on to another, the result being that neither cigarette nor filter is at all satisfactory; hence both are discarded with disgust. This is by no means the meaning I would have attached to the word *extension*, but I should prefer to have oral interpretation viewed as being concerned with the total range of literary study: that it serves to stretch literary study to its fullest, and that together oral interpretation and literary study make one exert oneself to full capacity. This is what I should like to have the word mean in this context.

I

Andor Gomme, in his book *Attitudes to Criticism*, says: "The fusion of situation, response and expression is the sign of a poet genuinely alive to his own experience, and it is the guarantee of the relevance and validity of his presentment of it for the world in general."[1] Here it seems to me is encapsulated the total range of literary study—the poet, his time and place, his life, his style, and his poem: Faulkner in Oxford, Mississippi, and his Yoknapatawpha Saga; Hawthorne in Salem, Massachusetts, and *The Scarlet Letter;* Robert Frost on his Vermont farms and *North of Boston*. Here are the poets responding to their situations and expressing themselves in their poems. Herein lies part of the total range of literary study which we said the interpreter must be concerned with: the poet, where he lived and at what time.

Another aspect of the total range of literary study with which the oral interpreter must concern himself—and this aspect may weigh a little heavier in the scale pan—is the poet's *expression* or style. (Henry James, in *The Scenic Art*, says that "the application of an art is style, and that style is expression, and that expression is the salt of life. . . .")

Let us, for purposes of illustration, take only two of the many facets of the poet's expression with which the interpreter must be vitally concerned: point of view, the perspective from which the story is seen; and diction, the poet's choice and use of words. And as examples let's use William Faulkner's "A Justice" and "Was," in my opinion two of the funniest stories in American literature.

"A Justice" is essentially the story of how Sam Fathers, one of the main characters in *The Bear*, got his name. (Among the Negroes he was called Uncle Blue-Gum; the white people called him Sam Fathers; but his real name, given to him by a Chickasaw chief, was Had-Two-Fathers!) The story begins with Quentin Compson, the hero of *The Sound and the Fury*, as narrator. But the job of narrator soon shifts to Sam Fathers, who is telling Quentin the tale of how he got his name as it was told to him by Herman Basket, a friend of Sam's father, Crawfish Ford, Craw-ford for short. Without question the oral reader must attend to these changes in narration, since they account for much of the humor and the shifts in tone of the story.

"Was" is the story of how Uncle Buck (Theophilus) McCaslin came to marry Miss Sophonsiba Beauchamp. As in "A Justice," where much of the humor was to be found in the use of point of view, Faulkner's use of language in "Was" accomplishes much the same purpose. The diction is precise, appropriate, vigorous, and evocative. Here, for example, is the scene in which Uncle Buck and McCaslin Edmonds are walking with Mr. Hubert Beauchamp towards his house, and Miss Sophonsiba, Mr. Hubert's maiden sister, comes onto the scene.

>But at last a hand began waving a handkerchief or something white through the broken place in an upstairs shutter. They went to the house, crossing the back gallery, Mr. Hubert warning them again, as he always did, to watch out for the rotted floor-board he hadn't got around to having fixed yet. Then they stood in the hall, until presently there was a jangling and swishing noise and they began to smell the perfume, and Miss Sophonsiba came down the stairs. Her hair was roached under a lace cap; she had on her Sunday dress and beads and a red ribbon around her throat and a little nigger girl carrying her fan and he stood quietly a step behind Uncle Buck, watching her lips until they opened and he could see the roan tooth. He had never known anyone before with a roan tooth....
>
>"Why, Mister Theophilus," she said. "And McCaslin," she said. She had never looked at him and she wasn't talking to him and he knew it, although he was prepared and balanced to drag his foot when Uncle Buck did. "Welcome to Warwick."
>
>He and Uncle Buck dragged their foot. "I just come to get my nigger," Uncle Buck said. "Then we got to get on back home."
>
>Then Miss Sophonsiba said something about a bumblebee, but he couldn't remember that. It was too fast and there was too much of it, the earrings and beads clashing and jingling like little trace chains on a toy mule trotting and the perfume stronger too, like the earrings and beads

sprayed it out each time they moved and he watched the roan-colored tooth flick and glint between her lips . . .[2]

Notice how skillfully Miss Sophonsiba's presence is made to seem almost overpowering for Uncle Buck and McCaslin by the repetition of the references to the beads, earrings, perfume, and that roan tooth, which in itself holds a great deal of fascination for the nine-year-old Cas Edmonds. There are other compelling features of the story that are the result of the author's diction. The story is full of images and terms relating to the sport of hunting—indeed the hunt becomes the controlling metaphor of the story. The oral interpreter must respond to the images and know the hunting terms if he is to project the rhythm and tone of the story. He may find it necessary to turn to his dictionary or some other source to find the meaning of such terms as "the fyce had faulted," "He's going to earth," "the hounds were cast," and should the reader not be satisfied with only a vague concept of the meaning of the word *roan*, he might discover even more humor in the additional connotations of the word.

II

You may recall that the second meaning given to extension was that oral interpretation served to stretch the study of literature to its fullest extent. By that I mean that the student must not only be able to recognize and define the devices of the writer's (poet's) craft, but that he must also understand *why* a particular poetic device is used. What does it do to amplify the emotional state of the speaker? Does it serve to intensify the excitement of the observer (audience)? Is it used to bring about a more definite empathic response by imitating the physical action of the experience? These are important questions that must be answered by one who attempts to give vocal and physical expression to the poem.

Why, for example, does Thomas à Becket in T. S. Eliot's *Murder in the Cathedral* ask the Fourth Tempter:

> Who are you, tempting with my own desires?
> Others have come, temporal tempters,
> With pleasure and power at palpable price.
> What do you offer? what do you ask?[3]

Do you suppose that Eliot was indulging himself? That he was engaged in an exercise in the use of alliteration, assonance, and consonance? I don't think so. I think that the deliberate repetition of the initial and medial plosive sounds at a fixed interval are used to underscore and amplify the emotional state of the speaker. The consonants' sounds echo the abnormally strong pulsing of the heart, the surge of blood, the fear of the speaker.

Robert Frost uses the same device but for a different effect in his poem "The Witch of Coos." You undoubtedly recall the story at the moment when the mother is aware that the cellar bones had mounted the stairs and were waiting helpless behind the door. The mother perceives that "The fainter and restless rustling ran all through them." Here the poet is using tone color to increase suspense and to create a ghost story atmosphere.

By the same token the oral interpreter must stretch his knowledge beyond the mere task of being able to recognize a particular metrical pattern. More importantly he must be sensible to the reasons why the pattern is regular or to those times when the pattern is broken. Once more let's take another of Frost's poems to illustrate our principle. In his poem "Two Tramps in Mud Time," the predominate pattern is four stressed syllables to the line. The central action of the poem is splitting wood. "Good blocks of beech it was I split, / As large around as the chopping block;. . . ." The swing of the ax and the muscular involvement are wonderfully captured by the stress pattern as illustrated in the following lines:

> You'd think I never had felt before
> The weight of an axhead poised aloft,
> The grip on earth of outspread feet
> The life of muscles rocking soft
> And smooth and moist in vernal heat.[4]

An interesting use of an irregular stress pattern is to be found in Shakespeare's *King Lear*, when the Old King wanders about in an open field during a thunderstorm and bellows, "Blow winds, and crack your cheeks! Rage! Blow!" Here the irregularity of the lines reflects the mental state of the character as well as the violence of the storm. Ernest M. Robson, in his interesting book *The Orchestra of the Language*, says: "The exclamatory breaks and changes in the pace of the speech not only direct the reader-listener's attention toward the outbursts of phonetic power that Shakespeare put into his words and syllables. They are signs of excitement and symbols of the broken fragmented emotions erupted in the explosion of Lear's mind. The phrase timing is Shakespeare the dramatist directing his actors to get across to the public the expressive power that Shakespeare the poet wrote into his words."[5]

III

Thus far I have attempted to show how oral interpretation is concerned with the total range of literary study and how it serves to stretch literary study to its fullest extent. At this point I should like to show how oral interpretation when based on solid literary study causes one to exert oneself to his fullest extent, and when that happens sheer joy is the result.

I have known a student who, when confronted with Karl Shapiro's poem "Christmas Eve: Australia," expressed anything but joy. Yet, when led through a careful study of the piece he showed signs of joy that came with discovery. First, he *really* became aware that a human being was caught up in a situation fraught with irony and humor. The speaker in the poem is a soldier who no doubt has been drafted into the army. He finds himself in a strange land where the wind blows hot on Christmas Eve. He is alone, surrounded by strangers. He does the things any soldier might do. He smokes, chews gum, reads his Bible, and thinks of Christ and Christmas of last year. The poem has touched the student's life in a very real way. His joy is further heightened when he becomes aware of the beautiful structure of the poem. Why, it's a sonnet! Now he is concerned with meter and rhyme. He responds to the change that occurs at the end of the octave and to the personal resolution that occurs in the last two lines of the sestet. He responds quite easily to the diction: it's so right. He feels the tensions that are inherent in the irony that runs all the way through the poem. Nothing is left now but to give the poem even more life through performance. Here is the opportunity to exert himself to his fullest capacity. He must achieve that fusion of situation, response, and expression. Perhaps this is what Northrop Frye means when he says

> What poetry can give the student is, first of all, the sense of physical movement. Poetry is not irregular lines in a book, but something very close to dance and song, something to walk down the street keeping time to. Even if the rhythm is free, it's still something to be declaimed. The surge and sweep of Homer and the sinewy springing rhythm of Shakespeare have much the same origin: they were written that way partly because they had to be bellowed at a restless audience. Modern poets work very hard at trying to convince people in cafes or even in parks on Sunday that poetry can be performed and listened to like a concert. There are quieter effects in poetry, of course, but a lot even of them have to do with physical

movement, such as the effect of wit that we get from strict meter, from hearing words stepping along in an ordered marching rhythm. . . .[6]

I have attempted to show that oral interpretation is an extension of literary study by the fact that it utilizes the total range of literary study, that it stretches literary study to its fullest capacity, and that it causes the interpreter to exert himself to the fullest capacity. I have also suggested that what the interpreter does with his voice and body in this act of extension is largely dictated by what he finds in his script. The end of the act, hopefully, is that the interpreter joins into a partnership with the poet to create a moment of joy.

Notes

1. Andor H. Gomme, *Attitudes to Criticism* (Carbondale: Southern Illinois University Press, 1966), p. 102.
2. William Faulkner, "Was." Copyright 1942 by William Faulkner. Reprinted from GO DOWN, MOSES by William Faulkner, by permission of Random House, Inc. Published in Great Britain by William Faulkner and reprinted by permission of the Author's Literary Estate and Chatto and Windus Ltd., London, England.
3. T. S. Eliot, *Murder in the Cathedral* (New York: Harcourt, Brace & World, Inc., 1952), p. 55.
4. From "Two Tramps in Mud Time" from COMPLETE POEMS OF ROBERT FROST. Copyright 1936 by Robert Frost. Copyright © 1964 by Lesley Frost Ballantine. Reprinted by permission of Holt, Rinehart and Winston Inc., and Jonathan Cape Limited and Laurence Pollinger Limited, London, England.
5. Ernest M. Robson, *The Orchestra of the Language* (Cranbury, N. J.: A. S. Barnes & Company, Inc. [Yoseloff]), p. 126.
6. Northrop Frye, *The Educated Imagination* (Bloomington: Indiana University Press, 1964), pp. 121-122.

form
Teaching Delivery Techniques of Oral Interpretation ● Willard J. Friederich

In the past few years I have sometimes had the uneasy feeling that the teaching of the oral interpretation of literature has been moving from the aegis of the speech department to the aegis of the English department—not, I hasten to add, at the request of, not because of pressure by, and perhaps not even with the realization of the various English departments. Rather, the move seems to be engineered by speech teachers themselves.

I'm not too sure what motivates such a possible trend. Perhaps a sincere belief by a teacher that his students need more help in analyzing a work than in orally presenting it, or that they acquire techniques of delivery more easily and quickly than the process of analysis. Perhaps the notion of some speech teachers (long plagued and still plagued by the beliefs of some of their colleagues that speech represents an inferior position in the roster of academic disciplines) that emphasis on literary analysis and criticism lends their course a stronger air of academic erudition, respect, substance, than does emphasis on a skill. Perhaps merely some teachers' inclination to minimize or avoid the trying days of repetitious drill necessary to develop mastery of voice and body in favor of, admittedly, more intellectually challenging, satisfying, even exciting days of analyzing literary form and content.

In any event, an increasing emphasis on literary analysis often seems to be coupled with a decreasing emphasis on oral presentation. Such adjustment in emphases, of course, is virtually inevitable: there is only so much time in any given term, and when the time devoted to any one element of a course is extended, something else in the course must give way.

Before I am suspected of advocating concentration on only the bare mechanics of delivery or mere performance gimmicks, to the neglect or even exclusion of meaning, thought, and perception, may I attest to the first prerequisite in any approach to teaching oral interpretation: the reader's need to thoroughly understand the literature to be shared with his audience. Skill without substance, form without content—if, indeed, such a condition is actually possible—is surely an empty feat. On the other hand, however, oral interpretation is a speech art. This label demands that a reader *convey* his understanding and appreciation of a literary work through his skill as a *speaker*. If it is true, and I believe it is, that a facile technician without grasp of the material amounts to little, it is equally true that a master scholar without the skill of communication will transmit very little to his audience. Both skill and understanding are necessary to bring a literary work to life through the ear.

I believe, therefore, that in the teaching of interpretation it is likewise necessary to give approximately equal emphasis to literary analysis and delivery. Perhaps it is only my foolish notion that in some schools the former is gradually outweighing or even virtually ousting the latter—at least in terms of class time devoted to each. True, I have little factual evidence to support my feeling. I have had no time to conduct a national survey and establish the usual all-important statistics. But every now and then, as I examine a recent article or book in oral interpretation, I get the impression I am reading an English text, not a speech text. The feeling grows when I talk with teachers or study syllabi from other schools. Above all, when some of my former students, as graduate assistants teaching the beginning interpretation course, tell me what and how they are directed to teach, I become most apprehensive.

Some time ago, for instance, I encountered a syllabus in which many days were scheduled for the oral and written analysis of a work and for each student's graded reading of that work—but not one day was specifically allocated to the theory and practice of how to transmit the feeling and thought the analysis had uncovered. And, in the end, a reader's failure or success in projecting the essence of a literary selection is largely dependent on his command of reading techniques that reveal what he knows. All I could ask at that point was, "But who teaches the kid to READ?"

At the graduate level such a course plan would make some sense, of course, since one would have every right to expect a properly prepared graduate student to know how to read effectively. But this is surely not true at the undergraduate level, especially in the beginning course. Indeed, with such a sequence of so-called basic courses as his background, how could even a graduate student fairly be expected to exhibit real competence, to say nothing of artistry? As has been said countless times, understanding alone does not insure effective oral reading.

However, I really am not pointing an accusing finger or trying to start a controversy. After all, I may be quite wrong, having misunderstood the facts or misinterpreted the signs. But one fact, I believe, is clear and does have a distinct bearing on our task. Regardless of whether literary analysis really is or is not squeezing delivery techniques out of some beginning interpretation courses, surely this situation should not be incorporated into a syllabus for a course in oral interpretation for prospective English teachers.

Overemphasis on literary analysis could perhaps be somewhat justified in a class of speech majors, who might be expected to have some knowledge of and experience in effective oral communication and, likewise, to be somewhat deficient in appreciation and understanding of literature. But the reverse should be true of a class of English majors. We should be able to assume a reasonable proficiency and experience in literary analysis and, thus, keep it to a minimum in this course. It also follows, then, that we should concentrate on delivery, an area where they could reasonably be expected to possess less experience and proficiency. Our job here is to set up a course to teach the student to transmit to others, through good oral reading, what he knows about his major field of the study of literature.

In line with this thought, therefore, I would urge that our adopted syllabus strongly stress delivery techniques. Much of the class discussion should concern ways and methods of projecting the thought and feeling of a selection through a responsive body and voice. Ungraded drills and exercises should be frequent, to allow and encourage the instructor to give all the practical help he can in how to read effectively. There should be specific instruction in cutting a selection, preparing the listeners to receive the selection, developing a real sense of sharing and communication, and so on.

Next, we should remember that the English teacher reading in the classroom is not a speech teacher reading in public, and the same standards need not necessarily apply, at least not in the same degree. The speech teacher, representing a reasonably standardized discipline and art form, has some professional obligation to keep within the recognized boundaries of that art—in short, to be a good example, a model of acceptable techniques in oral interpretation. Thus, for example, extremes in use of any techniques are usually questionable;

poetry should sound like poetry, not prose; informality will be more nearly formal than it might be in other circumstances; gimmicks to "startle and waylay" are rarely to be tolerated. And, though I dread even mentioning the old conflict of acting-versus-reading, I certainly believe that what we generally recognize and define as "acting" has no place in the interpreter's scope of reading techniques, though of course I recognize the debatable, fine line between the two in many cases. The speech teacher on the public platform, to conclude, has not only the goal of sharing his understanding and appreciation of a literary work with an audience that voluntarily came for that purpose but, like a concert singer or pianist, also has to represent the professional standards and highest dignity of his art.

The high school English teacher in his own classroom, however, is a horse of another color. His one purpose is to capture the attention and interest of his captive audience, to make "work" so fascinating that it seems desirable, even to those many students whose determination to reject it is almost a solemn duty because it is, after all, part of the "establishment." In my opinion, therefore, this teacher is free to use any techniques, even the slick gimmicks, that may achieve his goal. Anything that commands attention, produces thought and concentration, broadens understanding, evokes proper emotional response, illuminates meaning, deepens perception, or develops sensitivity is an effective technique, and, consequently, a justifiable technique. The teacher's job is to help youngsters—and youngsters of an era in which literature is probably the lowest notch on the totem pole when compared with TV, movies, folk rock, pot, and protest marches—to understand and, one hopes, enjoy literature and to develop the habit of reading. To achieve this goal with professional dignity and art is highly desirable, of course, and well worth a try. But achieve it he must; and if standing on his head will work when other techniques won't, then my only advice to him is to learn to stand on his head as quickly as possible! In other words, in these circumstances poetry may sound like poetry or prose, depending on what the goal is at that moment; informality and formality may lose many of their distinctions; overexaggeration may be the best or only way out; acting may illuminate more than subtly suggestive reading, and so on. Of what good is it to follow the "rules" and lose the victory?

The next question, therefore, should be, What does attract, stimulate, illuminate? In an attempt to get a firsthand answer, an audience preference ballot was taken at a reading program attended by about 250 people. The program was a theme program in which the reader used prose, poetry, and drama: some selections were the standard classics found in the typical textbooks, and some were simple modern pieces whose chief asset is the delineation of a character, painting of a mood, exploration of a contemporary theme, or merely the satirizing of a recent point of view for the fun of it.

The reader tried to demonstrate as many as possible degrees of what various people may call interpretation, ranging from pure acting to straight reading. The reader also tried to use a variety of delivery techniques: open and closed situations, manuscript and memorized reading, formal and informal atmosphere, placement of characters and no placement, simply suggested moods and moods theatricalized by special lighting and musical backgrounds. Formal readings were done behind the lectern, and informal readings were done walking about or sitting on a chair or stool and even on the edge of the stage apron. Some poetry, selected to that end, exaggerated a regularized meter; other poems treated content as in prose, ignoring meter for emphasis on thought and sentence structure, using only a mild overall pulse or virtually none at all. The speaker tried to demonstrate that characterization could be considered acting when the performer, discarding his manuscript, psychologically became the character in a scene created onstage around him, physically imitating the character; on the other hand, the speaker demonstrated that one could also "act" a character with manuscript in hand, moving or not moving, or that he could merely suggest a character, as a reader, both with and without a manuscript. Some characters were differentiated by extreme vocal manipulation and use of dialects; some were presented in the reader's own voice, without characterizing variations.

The audience members were asked to vote for the techniques they liked best, having also the opportunity to indicate no preference. Of the completed, valid ballots, 33 percent were written by adults, 29 percent by college students, and 38 percent by high school students. The results were often surprisingly similar among the three groups; but, since we are now concerned with high school students and their attitudes, I shall deal with their responses only.

Slightly over half of them preferred open situations. Forty percent preferred material to be memorized, though 44 percent had no preference either way. Overwhelmingly (84 percent), they liked an informal atmosphere. Thirty-six percent preferred emphasis on the rhythm of poetry, 42 percent emphasis on content to the subordination of rhythm, and 22 percent had no strong preference. Again overwhelmingly (94 percent), they wanted characters vocally differentiated, and also placed (71 percent). Sixty-one percent liked the speaker to be the character, 24 percent liked him to merely suggest the character, and 14 percent would accept either. The majority warmed to what might be called "dramatic effects," 53 percent enjoying musical backgrounds and 73 percent lighting effects to heighten mood. Although such devices would rarely be available to a teacher in an average English classroom, they were included in the experiment in an attempt to measure the possible extent of emotional stimuli to which an audience might favorably respond. When asked to indicate which numbers on the program they would omit if given a chance, their only significant choice (28 percent) was Shakespeare, though 10 percent also chose to omit two of the poems. Not surprisingly, they cared for poetry less than for prose and prose drama; but, more surprisingly, they had far fewer objections than one might perhaps expect from youngsters of this age.

General conclusions to be drawn from these figures are not too absolute, of course (if absolute conclusions could ever be drawn from only one experiment), because it is highly unlikely that anyone can completely divorce his response to technique of delivery from his response to the selection itself. Thus, it seems impossible to ever be sure just how precisely he is measuring one element to the exclusion of the other. Even so, several responses seem worthy of contemplation. The classroom teacher can certainly take advantage of student interest in an open situation and informal atmosphere, both of them closely allied with the classroom situation. Poetry is still the big obstacle course, and the prospective teacher had better try his best to learn to master its music as well as its meaning if he wishes to reach his students. In any material in which characterization is prominent, the students want, at the least, clear-cut vocal and physical suggestion of characters; and apparently the majority prefer the extremes of characterization, what most of us would probably call acting, or at least the next thing to it. Anything the teacher can do to help them experience the "dramatic" mood and tension of a selection is clearly welcome.

To provide the most help to the prospective teacher, therefore, I would conclude that the syllabus for a one-semester course should make every effort, insofar as the dire limitations of only one semester will allow, to include the following major aspects:

1. The use of the voice: color words, connotations, contrasts, speech pattern, emphasis, articulation.

2. Physical response: muscular reaction, eye contact, inner tension.
3. The author's attitude, as revealed in voice and body: emotional key.
4. The rhythm of poetry, as transmitted by the voice: beat and pulse, phrasing, tempo, vowel duration, pause.
5. Characterization, as suggested through voice and body: variety, placement, motivation, timing, rhythm.

Time to treat all these aspects, of course, will be a major obstacle to overcome. By using traditional selections that any English majors should be completely familiar with through regular English courses, much time normally spent on content analysis could be saved. The metrical analysis of well-known poems should be virtually unnecessary.

Using many short exercises can cover much ground in the least amount of time and give each student a varied amount of experience. In approaching English composition, for example, one learns to write a good sentence, then to put sentences together in a logical paragraph, finally to organize the paragraphs into a coherent theme; but there is no point in trying a theme until one can write a sentence. So, in interpretation, one must consider choice, denotation and connotation of words; phrasing as the unit of thought; interrelationships of words, phrases, sentences, and paragraphs; and so forth—and all such implications must be transmitted to the listener by a flexible, responsive voice. Going beyond meaning, one must further project, vocally and physically, the author's attitude or tone. All these considerations are as prevalent in well-selected sentences and short paragraphs as they are in full essays, stories, or poems. A beginner, therefore, can learn these principles and develop his vocal and physical responsiveness by working on such short practice selections. In fact, vocal variety and flexibility may be greatly improved by the simple exercise of saying a list of "color" words in such a way that the speaker suggests or underlines the meaning and emotional connotation of each word. Just as the beginning pianist masters his scales and chords before he attempts Chopin, so the reader can sharpen his techniques before he tries to sustain longer pieces of literature. The same is true of developing vocal and physical techniques for characterizing the people in drama and prose.

In poetry the additional problems of meter and rhythm likewise require much practice. Choral speaking of short poems can give all in the class elementary drill in rhythm, vowel duration, and phrasing at the same time. I am not speaking of choral speaking as a polished art form, of course, but merely as a means to the end of learning the difficult techniques of reading poetry. All in the class can get the most experience in the least amount of time by working on the same nongraded practice selection, thus necessitating only one analysis and making all the instructor's suggestions applicable to everybody.

Undoubtedly, these teaching methods and other similar ones are well known and often used by teachers of interpretation. But my point is that, if a student is in just one semester to get adequate training in the basic reading techniques he will need, a workable syllabus can be built perhaps only on such time-saving devices. Finally, by limiting the size of the class to about fifteen students, there is a reasonable hope that this course might help the prospective English teacher to make literature come alive through the ears of his students.

A Supervisor Looks at the Teaching of Literature in the High School ● Clarence W. Hach

As a supervisor of English in a high school, I have for many years observed the teaching of literature in the classroom and have sensed the differences made by a teacher's ability to read well orally. I have also observed the difference made by a teacher's knowledge of such oral interpretation techniques as choric speech, readers or chamber theatre, or even a teacher's ability to teach pupils themselves to read well aloud. As a result, I have often seen the difference between a pupil's real enjoyment and appreciation of literature and his lack of it. As a supervisor I have tried to recommend for employment teachers who have had course work in oral interpretation. I have also recommended such work to those teachers planning further graduate work, particularly those wishing to work toward a sixth year of academic preparation, which in our school does not mean just thirty more hours of graduate work. The philosophy behind our sixth year is that course work should be pointed toward making a teacher more effective in the work he is doing. Courses contemplated must be discussed with the department supervisor and receive approval from the Sixth Year Committee, a small interpepartmental group of classroom teachers and supervisors, and the superintendent. We are fortunate in Evanston, of course, in having Northwestern University's excellent department of oral interpretation easily accessible so that teachers wishing to take work can readily do so, particularly during the summer session.

As a supervisor of English, I know that I look at the teaching of literature differently from many, particularly those department chairmen and teachers of English in schools in which such traditional courses as American, English, and world literature are still taught, and taught traditionally, particularly where they are taught with a general anthology providing the core reading. The emphases in those schools, whether stated or not, are generally not on literature itself but rather on literary chronology, historical and social aspects, the transmission of the cultural heritage, literary movements, and the like. To be convinced one need only look at the kinds of examinations given, whether teacher or department made. Someone once said that the single best way of determining what a teacher considers important is to look at his examinations. I know that I agree. More than I like to think, literature examinations in the United States too often deal with what someone has called the "trappings" of literature rather than with the literature itself.

What should be the major emphases in the teaching of literature in today's high schools? I think that there are two:

First, and most important, is the enjoyment and appreciation of literature, of reading itself. If our pupils do not learn to enjoy and appreciate literature, we are failures as teachers of literature. With the great variety of pupils who attend today's comprehensive high schools, we cannot have the same kind of literature program for all pupils, not if we consider enjoyment and appreciation our number one emphasis. Not every pupil can read and enjoy Joseph Conrad's *Victory*; not every one can appreciate *Gulliver's Travels*, no matter how capable the teacher. Not every senior can enjoy and appreciate the poetry of Byron, Shelley, or Keats. Not every pupil should have the kind of literature program usually taught in courses labeled American or English literature.

Not very many weeks ago I observed in a nearby suburban high school a very capable young teacher attempting to teach Byron's poem "Don Juan" to a noncollege bound, lower-average group of seniors. As the teacher explained all of the allusions in the poem, the class was polite, because I sensed that they liked this teacher. She tried her best to make the poem relevant to their lives by relating it to current problems in Greece, but despite her best efforts and, I might add, her good oral reading ability, the poem was not right for this class, and there wasn't that which I consider essential for enjoyment and appreciation—an emotional and intellectual interaction between the reader and the work of art. The poem was entirely too difficult for this class. It was taught primarily because it was in the text being used in a course in English literature.

I really believe that these traditional courses traditionally taught do more to turn pupils away from good reading than to it, that few pupils become what I like to think should be a major goal of our literature courses—and that is helping pupils to become compulsive readers, young people who must read to survive. I really believe that many English teachers, despite their best intentions, have done more to develop nonreaders than they have to develop compulsive readers. Despite the importance of the cultural heritage and everything else associated with good reading, unless our pupils really become, to paraphrase one of Dan Fader's titles, "hooked on reading," little else that we do in teaching literature matters. Our number one job is to "hook" young people on reading so that they will continue to read all of their adult lives.

If we give top priority to this objective, it precludes our teaching many traditional titles to all of our young people. It precludes the traditional kinds of literature programs dictated by general anthologies. It invites a diversified program in literature that will appeal to pupils of wide ability and many backgrounds. It makes extremely important, in choosing what literature to teach, that which is or can be relevant to young people *now*. It does not necessarily mean their reading only contemporary literature, of course, for to include only that would mean to ignore much which is universal and perhaps to emphasize only the ephemeral. It might mean for some pupils getting at *Romeo and Juliet* through *West Side Story*. It can mean teaching *Huckleberry Finn* to all but the most nonacademic, those with severe reading problems. It can mean teaching such novels as *The Caine Mutiny* and *The Ox-Bow Incident* to some rather than those novels in the usual *belles lettres* tradition. It certainly means having a teacher who can read literature well himself and who understands how to use techniques of oral interpretation to create more interest in the literature being read or to enable pupils to appreciate even more that literature in which they already have an interest.

The second major emphasis in teaching literature, I believe, is to teach pupils to read with understanding—in other words, to improve their ability to read per se. Because teaching pupils how to look at a piece of literature, how to see what is there, how to discover what it means is a gradual process, and because learning is a growth process, a literature program must be sequentially arranged so that a pupil progresses throughout his years in high school to increasingly mature reading. Most high school literature programs that I know anything about are really not organized in this way. If short stories, for example, are taught, every year from the ninth to the twelfth grades, those in the tenth grade aren't necessarily more complex than those in the ninth or less complex than those in the eleventh. Ability to read short stories at the tenth grade level does not necessarily depend upon having learned to read those at the ninth. The same criticism can be leveled at the other genres—poetry, the novel, drama, and nonfiction.

"If literature is a subject matter," according to the course of study of one school system that really has a meaningful sequential program in literature, "there should be something progressive about the learning of literature. This progression can be seen as a passing from the study of the relatively simple to the relatively complex, always," of course, "keeping in mind the necessity for selecting important, worthwhile works," works that can be interesting and relevant to pupils. "The chief guidepost which helps to differentiate the simple from the complex is the movement from external to internal," according to the course of study of the Tamalpais Union High School District of California. "If we apply this idea to such familiar aspects of literature as structure, character, theme, and ideology, we can see that in the simpler works the emphasis is on action, incident, physical conflict; the characters are delineated through a description of external details; the theme or thesis is explicitly stated; and the view of human nature is somewhat static and conventional. But in the more complex work the emphasis is on the symbolic, or recurring patterns and heightened moments of awareness; the characters are delineated through an investigation of their internal states; the theme is multiple and is implied; and the mysterious, elusive quality of human nature is stressed. This description suggests another guiding principle: the intensification of the aspects of reality is a feature of the more complex work."

Because almost all structural elements present in other forms are present in the short story in capsule, in a developmental English program the short story is most appropriately placed and taught first so that a class may use its common elements for definition, development, and departure in subsequent literary forms. To justify this kind of sequence, I suppose that an appropriate analogy would be to say that the short story is to a novel as a paragraph is to a full-length composition. That analogy may be somewhat faulty, I know, but I do think that it has value in thinking about the organization of a literature program based upon sound educational theory.

To take one structural element and arrange it on a continuum of complexity, let us take *conflict*. The simplest is usually man against man or man against nature, the next man in conflict with his environment, then conflict between intangible forces, and finally man against himself. Another element, the time factor, can be arranged from the natural chronological sequence to that not strictly chronological, perhaps with flashbacks, to the story in which time is relative. Similar continuums can be worked out for other structural elements of action and time as well as for setting, characterization, point of view, style, and theme. Using this description in its broadest sense, the Tamalpais course of study attempts a continuum of structural complexity in order to designate stories and places them on the high school grade levels. Because, of course, in any good short story some structural parts will move toward the extremes of the scale, those stories set on the continuum for grades 9-12 represent in their placement only the majority of the characteristics or their distinguishing features.

You might be interested in a specific application of one continuum as worked out in the Tamalpais course of study to show how the process of analysis, beginning with structure, leads to meaning. One unit is based on the structural element of the agent or character or protagonist or hero with the sequence of increasing difficulty ranging from the representative and external to the unique, internal, and yet universal. In the ninth grade we have the picaresque hero who moves from place to place chronologically but whose experiences do not greatly change him inwardly. The energy of the work derives from physical movement in time and place. Specific titles listed include, as a short story, "After Twenty Years" by William Sydney Porter; as a novel, *The Adventures of Huckleberry Finn*; as a play, *A Midsummer Night's Dream*; and as a poem, "Lord Randall."

At the tenth grade, the same inwardness is revealed in the characters, but they now move in a community-society as well as from place to place. Some of the energy derives from evocation of place. The short story cited is "Paul's Case"; the novel, *Arrowsmith*; the play, *Cyrano de Bergerac*; and the poem, "The Eve of St. Agnes."

In the eleventh grade the work derives its power-energy-charge from what goes on inside the hero who internalizes his awareness of the external human community. At this level the short story is "The Secret Sharer"; the novel, *Pride and Prejudice*; the play, *Oedipus Rex*; and the poem, "Mending Wall."

At the twelfth grade, within a unique individual the external and internal gain magnitude, scope, and intensity; and the external is embraced. The poet gives form to the persistent gestures of the soul. Interestingly, the short story cited is "Billy Budd"; the novel, *Passage to India*; the play, *Hamlet*; and the poem, "Ode on a Grecian Urn."

As a supervisor, I find this kind of analysis useful in curriculum building, particularly if one is attempting to build a developmental literature program based partly upon the fact that learning is a gradual growth process and, therefore, that a pupil's ability to read certain literary works depends partly upon what he has read and should be pointed toward what he will read.

The sequence I cited from the Tamalpais course of study is a sequential one on the basis of difficulty dealing with one structural element. Of course, it is also sequential when many other elements are considered. It is, however, only one sequence of titles, a sequence that is not appropriate for every pupil. If the sequence is to be meaningful, some titles would have to vary for different ability groups. Some pupils might be able to go through the ninth and tenth grade titles as given but would need to have other titles less difficult in other structural aspects than those cited for grades 11 and 12, not only less difficult structurally but more meaningful ideationally. What I really am saying is that what is needed in a high school literature program is sequences, not a sequence, so that all pupils can experience the enjoyment of literature at whatever ability level they happen to be and, too, so that all may progress gradually toward becoming more mature readers, again of the type of literature that is within their grasp. I think that Browning's words—"A man's reach should exceed his grasp"—are an appropriate guideline in planning a literature program so that titles, of whatever genre, are those that need to be taught in order for a pupil to understand them and therefore enjoy and appreciate them. If a title can be read and understood without any teaching, then I think that title should not be in a literature program. That is the kind of title that a pupil can read on his own in a free or personal reading program.

The kind of literature program I've been talking about is the kind that applies Jerome Bruner's statement in *The Process of Education*: "To be in command of these basic ideas, to use them effectively, requires a continual deepening of one's understanding of them that comes from learning to use them in progressively complex forms."[1]

In *Freedom and Discipline in English*, the report of the Commission on English of the College Entrance Examination Board, the usual ways of setting up a course in literature are discussed: the chronological-historical survey, the thematic approach, and that by literary types.[2] Whereas each has advantages and none is free from pitfalls and all will work with skillful teachers, total organization by literary types or genres is, as I see it, probably the most effective in meeting the two major emphases that a high school literature program should have—(1) that of helping pupils to interact emotionally and intellectually with a work of art so that they will become compulsive readers and (2) that of teaching pupils to read increasingly mature literature to the maximum of their ability.

According to *Freedom and Discipline in English*, "The advantages of this method [the genre approach] are that it forces the student to look upon literature as literature, not as an adjunct to philosophy, psychology, or the social studies. It invites the student to discover the variety and range possible within each type at the same time as he becomes increasingly aware of the inescapable limitations that each form imposes upon the writer. The hazard is juiceless formalism and an excessive preoccupation with terminology and analysis. Attention to form, however, is not pointless, and usually analysis must precede integrated understanding. In fact, most of what a teacher can teach and a student can learn about literature is form—the rhetorical and structural means by which literature achieves its ends. A gradually acquired and widely used vocabulary of rhetorical and formal terms, therefore, is an essential tool in the process of analysis and synthesis, which, in turn, leads to critical understanding. If we know, for example, that 'When to the sessions of sweet silent thought' begins a sonnet, . . . we bring to our reading of it certain expectations about its form, even about its sentiments, which are indispensable to understanding and appreciation. Knowledge of formal elements of literary work is presumably a large part of every English teacher's experience, and it is a knowledge he alone can transmit to students. Those elements do not constitute the whole of literature, but they are what distinguish it from other writing, and they must be taught if literature is to be seriously taught at all."[3]

It is this approach to literature that I believe is most essential to the oral interpretation of literature. That the reader may recreate for the listener the intent and the accomplishment of the author, he must understand the form and content of his selection. Oral interpretation demands intimate analysis of literature. A teacher who can teach pupils how to look at a piece of literature, how to see what is there, and how to discover what it means has an added skill of great value if he can read literature well. It is a further approach to the understanding of literature, which is essential to appreciation and enjoyment and to the acquisition of those skills important to the mature reading of literature.

Notes

1. Jerome S. Bruner, *The Process of Education* (Cambridge: Harvard University Press, 1960).

2. Commission on English, *Freedom and Discipline in English* (New York: College Entrance Examination Board, 1965).
3. *Ibid.*, p. 53.

Readers Theatre and the Short Story • Elizabeth Worrell

Once upon a time there was a teacher with a class of students, and they were "studying literature." They read, and they analyzed, and they discussed—at least the teacher discussed, and the students supposedly listened. Then the teacher made out a list of questions on what he thought they should know about the story, and the students tried to answer the questions the way they thought he wanted them answered, and everyone passed the course. Some of the students graduated to teaching classes just like this class, and some raised children who would take classes just like this one, and some took classes where they never had to read a short story, or even a poem or a novel, again. And they all lived happily ever after.

That is a true story—all except the ending. The ending was put in to please the principal, the parents, and maybe the teacher himself. Obviously this conference met because we recognize too many classes that resemble the one described. The teachers of literature are turning to speech activities for help, just as the oral interpreter has turned to a deeper study of literature to strengthen his own performance.

In his excellent book, *The Teaching of High School English*, J. N. Hook urges, not more, but more challenging activities in teaching literature and suggests oral reading as one of them. He recognizes, as do others, that "Often the understanding and appreciation of literature may be improved by oral reading."[1] Dr. Hook is for the most part talking of the individual reader. John Dixon, in his report based on the 1966 Dartmouth Seminar, urges group activity. "Where some students sit back," he says, "while a group presents a piece of drama, there is an opportunity for the teacher to draw from an audience an appreciation of what was enjoyed, of what went home, and thus confirm in the individual writer or group a sense of shared enjoyment and understanding."[2] Mr. Dixon recommends "drama," by which he means "doing, acting things out rather than working on them in abstract and in private." It is, he assures teachers, "the truest form of learning, for it puts knowledge and understanding to their test in action."[3]

Although many of the leading teachers of literature are urging the use of oral reading and acting, it is the oral interpretation teachers who call attention to readers theatre as an effective method of stimulating genuine response to literature. The authors of *Readers Theatre Handbook* recommend their text "to the teacher of English who wishes to vitalize his teaching by approaching literature orally and to stimulate his students not only to analyze a text but to experience it by vocally and physically embodying it."[4]

I am not recommending a fad in literature study, nor a glib and superficial approach to this important subject. Nor am I advocating group reading because it is easy, or because it will be an inexpensive way to produce a play. Such an attitude would be to the detriment of all concerned, including the authors. For the moment at least, I am discussing classroom performance, not public reading. Furthermore, I am not suggesting that the readers plunge into reading without analysis and preparation but rather that the two methods, analysis and oral interpretation, be blended. Readers theatre is not just oral storytelling, nor is it a group of people sitting in a circle—or a straight line—mumbling parts from a play. Rather, through discerning selection of what is to be read, recognition of the literary elements involved, sensitive arrangement of parts for the readers, and interaction of these readers, readers theatre can and should become a literary journey, hazardous it is true, but stimulating and infectiously exciting.

John Dixon warns the teacher of literature to avoid setting aside fragmented periods for speech activities. It may be that in the combination reading-analysis which readers theatre makes possible, a synthesis and understanding in depth can be most effectively achieved. Apathy and "dead end" experience have less chance in a classroom where each student has an investment in the activity.

The short story seems the ideal literary form to choose for a beginning experiment in readers theatre, for readers theatre is by nature experimental—in fact, teachers are encouraged to experiment. David Thompson points out that "each story prescribes its own attitudes."[5] Wallace Bacon, always encouraging, says of readers theatre, "There are no set inflexible rules. . . . There are conventions (though they must not be rigid), and there are outer limits (though they are not easy to define)."[6]

The short story is a literary form which, by its nature, seems perfectly suited to this flexibility of performance, for as Peden and other authorities on the story have said, it "eludes strict definition and defies attempts at arbitrary classification."[7] Those of us who believe that there are many ways to analyze a work of art will feel comfortable with the readers theatre method of presenting this versatile literary form.

There are many other reasons, of varying importance, for using the short story for classroom performance. The brevity of the form makes it efficient for classroom use, and because of its brevity it is selective in its material. (The necessary cutting and arrangement should make the student further aware of this selectivity.) In *The Lonely Voice*, an unusual study of the short story, Frank O'Connor says, "Since a whole lifetime must be crowded into a few minutes, these minutes must be carefully chosen indeed and lit by an unearthly glow, one that enables us to distinguish present, past and future as though they were all contemporaneous."[8] Because the story is compressed, the author must express much more than is actually said, using suggestion and symbolism as a part of the meaning of the story. This suggestive style in turn makes demands on both reader and listener. "The compression by suggestion and implication" Sean O'Faolain feels to be "one of the great charms of the short story."[9] The author's use of time frequently offers the greatest challenge in the study of compact fiction. How does he create "Time present and time past . . . and time future contained in time past"? Symbols of sea, river, birds, and wind occur and reoccur to enrich the texture of the writing and ultimately, it is hoped, affect the tone and tempo of the readers. The brevity of the story is directly related to the struggle with time. It is no accident that so many stories begin with the phrase "Once upon a time . . ."

In a class of, say, thirty students with almost as many different tastes, temperaments, and even experiences, the variety of theme and subject matter to be found in short stories is fortunate for teacher and students. From Gogol to Eudora Welty, from the story of Ruth to "A Rose for Emily," an assortment of characters wander over territory from Yoknapatawpha County to Kilimanjaro. What stories to select for oral reading need be no great problem. There are dozens of fine anthologies on the market, most of them with useful introductions on the short story. Dr. Coger in *Readers Theatre Handbook* makes practical suggestions for script material. Dwight Burton includes a helpful list of collections of short stories in *Literature Study in the High Schools*.[10] The teacher should make a number of collections available to the students—Peden, Mark Schorer, and others—so they may have a part in the project from the very first.

For a teacher and class having their initial experience with readers theatre, perhaps the first thing to do, after reading several stories and selecting one to read aloud, is to find out what to look for in the story. The Brooks and Warren volume, *Understanding Fiction*, would be a clear guide.[11] There are many others, of course, some already suggested. The teacher should choose the ones *he* finds interesting and most helpful.

A story has been chosen—perhaps it is "A Good Man Is Hard to Find," "Young Goodman Brown," or "The Use of Force"—what next? Should the teacher begin with the usual discussion of literary elements—plot, character, setting, theme? He may wish to do so, of course. But for some stories a study of point of view may serve as a strong motivating force for the reader to become involved in what is read. Point of view can place the class immediately in a discussion to determine the arrangement of the story for oral reading. Sooner or later class and teacher must decide how the narration is to be handled. "The nature of the narrator," Dr. Bacon reminds us, "is a crucial question for the interpreter."[12] Problems involving the oral narrator and point of view are often best considered together. Will the teacher use more than one narrator in reading the story? Will they speak in chorus or solo? How will he place them—if two, one on either side of the reading area? Or will a narrator move about among the characters? Does the single narrator read any of the roles in the story? In one arrangement of Virginia Woolf's "The Legacy," the narrator stood behind the husband, often seeming to prompt his thoughts, or at times to serve as a goad to his awakening conscience. In "A Rose for Emily," several "neighbors" acted as town gossips to tell the story. In "The Invisible Boy," the two characters gave the story without use of the narrator at all, using the indirect discourse sometimes as direct discourse, sometimes as stream-of-consciousness. The effect was frequently humorous, often poignant. (Using description and some narrative as direct discourse often helps to combat the tendency of the careless reader to skip everything that is not in quotation marks! Readers should be guided in such uses by the style of the story.)

By now the story should begin to take shape as a script for oral reading. The class turns to a consideration of the characters next. How do they know what a character is like? They should note the relationship to the other characters. As the readers begin to read aloud, the reaction of characters to and upon each other should develop. The rhythm of the story may begin to be felt and established. Perhaps at this point the readers will feel the need to examine the characters' reactions to environment. In some stories, such as "The Fall of the House of Usher," environment and mood may need to be recognized first. By now the class and their teacher probably have determined the theme, particularly if it is obviously stated; but obvious or not, they should take time now for reevaluation. For instance, is the theme of "The Man Who Loved His Kind," by Virginia Woolf, a study of the English social system? Is it the conflict between rich and poor? Is it the dichotomy of good and evil? Or is it all of these with the overlying theme of the difficulties of understanding each other as ironically implied in the title? This brings the class neatly to an investigation of irony which is so often found in the short story, thus introducing another element of fiction to be recognized, interpreted, responded to.

The word *conflict* appears often in discussions of fiction, and no effective readers theatre is likely to be without it. Even in a seemingly simple story such as Jarrell's *The Bat Poet*, the conflicting attitudes of the animals toward poetry move the plot along, motivate much of the action. In "The Invisible Boy," the conflict *is* the action. In "A Perfect Day for Bananafish," it lurks below the surface of the story only to emerge sharply at the end.

Before the final arrangement of the script, the reader must determine the various literary elements involved and which one is to be stressed in a given story. Brooks and Warren emphasize that the way to understand a piece of fiction is "by understanding the functions of the various elements which go to make up fiction and by understanding their relationship to each other in the whole construct." Class involvement and final emotional response to the story depend upon the "effect of the elements interacting with each other."[13] Sometimes a simple device will help establish character, provide a part of the environment, precipitate conflict, underline irony, and indicate the outcome, all in one story. Such a device is the mother's hat in Flannery O'Connor's "Everything That Rises Must Converge." The hat serves as a *motif* running through the story from the moment when it is first described as new, and we are told it cost seven dollars and a half—a hideous green and purple affair, "less comical," the son thinks, "than jaunty and pathetic." It is the hat that precipitates the bitter quarrel we hear between mother and son before they start to town. When the huge Negro woman gets on the bus, she is wearing an identical hat; "Julian saw that [the mother] and the woman had, in a sense, swapped sons. Though his mother would not realize the symbolic significance of this, she would feel it." After the mother is hit by the woman, the hat falls off, and later the son tells her cruelly, "It looked better on her than it did on you." When the story was given as readers theatre, no props or costumes were used, but the girls who read the mother and the woman were *aware* of those hats and the audience accepted them as real. They became more believable than actual hats ever could have.

The question arises: How does one stage readers theatre? As Dr. Bacon says, "There are conventions," and he clearly states these conventions in *The Art of Interpretation*. Comparable descriptions and suggestions are given in other interpretation texts and in articles in the *Quarterly Journal of Speech*. Ultimately the decisions must be the teacher's and the participating students', but they will be aided in their decisions by the literary critics and oral interpreters—and *by the literature itself*. Dr. Coger feels that the trend is toward greater freedom in presentation, more movement, less use of lecterns and readers' stools. Often props and a suggestion of costume are used. However, many directors believe that a minimum use of scenery, props, and costumes, and the readers' unobtrusive and skillful use of the book, help to keep the focus where it belongs—on the literature itself. An opportunity to help in planning the script, blocking whatever action may be used, and finding solutions to questions of interpretation that arise may stimulate the otherwise dormant imagination of a one-time disinterested student.

There are numerous aspects of the short story that will concern the group which we have not had time to mention. Almost nothing has been said here about oral and visual techniques—focus, use of pause, gesture in both language and action. No final answers have been given or positive recommendations made, but the absence of a definite solution or answer may challenge and intrigue the student in a way that an "end-stop" assignment never could.

While some members of the class are readers, what are the listeners doing? It is hoped that from the first they have all been involved in the planning, from selection of the story, through analysis and arrangement, to casting. Often a suggestion is made for a fellow classmate to read a particular role. A teacher may even stand a chance of being nominated for a part, such as the title role of the spider in *Charlotte's Web* or Dame Lettice in Muriel Spark's "The Interview." Then while one group reads, the other may become a critical audience and should, as Langston Hughes' friend Simple said, "Listen fluently." If the listeners are to speak with any fluency about what they observe, they will need a vocabulary for expressing themselves with accuracy and confidence. Brooks and Warren, Timko and Oliver, Bacon, and others provide brief but serviceable glossaries of critical terms.

If much of what has been said here sounds like a familiar echo of what has been read and heard elsewhere, it is because that is the way it is. No doubt readers have also recognized that a number of the ideas have come from students in both literature and oral interpretation classes.

Although my primary interest has focused on classroom discussion and performance, reading for additional audiences can provide further motivation for student work. Readings for other literature classes, assemblies, and clubs may expand the circle of interest and appreciation of literature in school and community. Whether the experience goes beyond the classroom or not, at least one can be sure the stories have been read, and it seems possible that some of them will be remembered and even understood!

The only way to make a continuing reader out of anyone of any age is through sensitive selection and vitality of method to get the individual, and his friends as well, *involved* in the literature. Readers theatre may be just the method that could work. A short story or poem, by its very brevity, may slip in and out of a boy's mind as easily as a fish in water. But if there is something about the moment of seeing the fish—a splash of sun or a shifting shadow—or about the setting in which it is perceived (the slope of shore or vibration of the pond), the experience of the fish may stay in the consciousness of the boy until he is as old as Johnny Pye. The problem the teacher must continue to explore is how to recognize—and hold—the moment!

A teacher should give his students a voice in what they read and how they will read it. It may take more patience, more work for both teacher and students. The teacher will be plagued by frustration and sometimes failure. He must not give up. Young people today are making it increasingly clear they want a part in decision making. The teacher's role, among others he must play, is to help equip them for decisions. In a recent article for *Life*, history professor James Billington wrote, "Joy in posing and solving questions for oneself may help one to create fewer problems for others."[14]

Suppose now we rewrite the story with which we began, using the same setting and characters, but an altered plot. The story is read, the discussion starts, but this time differently, because now students and teacher alike have an immediate and recognizable goal in view. They study the story in order to participate in it. Together they recreate what they have read. This time, however, there is no "happy" ending—in fact, let us hope that there is no "ending" at all, but a continuing experience in literature as students and teacher chart their passage on a voyage of discovery.

Anyone can start on such a voyage with comparative safety; all he needs is a good boat, a steady compass, a patient captain, and a willing crew. *Bon voyage!*

Notes

1. J. N. Hook, *The Teaching of High School English* (3rd ed.; New York: The Ronald Press Company, 1965), p. 427.
2. John Dixon, *Growth through English*: A Report Based on the Dartmouth Seminar, 1966 (Reading, England: National Association for the Teaching of English, 1967), p. 8.
3. *Ibid.*, p. 43.
4. Leslie Irene Coger and Melvin R. White, *Readers Theatre Handbook: A Dramatic Approach to Literature* (Glenview, Ill.: Scott, Foresman and Company, 1967), Preface.
5. David W. Thompson and Virginia Fredericks, *Oral Interpretation of Fiction: A Dramatistic Approach* (2nd ed.; Minneapolis: Burgess Publishing Company, 1964), p. 80.
6. Wallace A. Bacon, *The Art of Interpretation* (New York: Holt, Rinehart and Winston, Inc., 1966), p. 306.
7. William Peden (ed.), *Twenty-nine Short Stories* (Boston: Houghton Mifflin Company, 1960), p. vii.
8. Frank O'Connor, *The Lonely Voice: A Study of the Short Story* (New York: World Publishing Company, 1965), p. 22.
9. Sean O'Faolain, "On Convention," in *Thirty-eight Short Stories: An Introductory Anthology*, ed. Michael Timko and Clinton F. Oliver (New York: Alfred A. Knopf, Inc., 1968), p. 34.
10. Dwight L. Burton, *Literature Study in the High Schools* (Rev. ed.; New York: Holt, Rinehart and Winston, Inc., 1967), pp. 182-184.
11. Cleanth Brooks and Robert Penn Warren, *Understanding Fiction* (2nd ed.; New York: Appleton-Century-Crofts, 1959).
12. Bacon, *The Art of Interpretation*, p. 376.
13. Adrian H. Jaffe and Virgil Scott (eds.), *Studies in the Short Story* (3rd ed.; New York: Holt, Rinehart and Winston, Inc., 1968), p. 12.
14. James H. Billington, "The Humanistic Heartbeat Has Failed," *Life*, May 24, 1968, pp. 32-35.

Why Read to High School Students? Vernell G. Doyle

A retiring grade school superintendent told me recently that once upon a time reading aloud to a class was not considered good instruction and was not done. That time must have been long ago. While reading in preparation for this conference, I found the following recognition and recommendation concerning the secondary school teacher of English and oral interpretation in *Talks to Beginning Teachers of English* by Dorothy Dakin. "Part of the equipment of a teacher of English is ability to read, by which I do not mean declamatory or dramatic expression, but simple interpretation of thought. If you do not read aloud well, take a course in interpretative reading and practice as much as possible." The book that contained the above directive was published in 1937.

The superintendent, in addition to telling me that he now considered reading aloud to be a good practice, expressed a reason for reading aloud: "You can't skip any words." In today's world of skimming and speed reading and *Reader's Digest* condensations, I suppose many words are skipped, and enjoyment and understanding are diminished. By reading aloud, we might bring students in contact with words they might skip.

I'm not sure that getting all the words is the most important reason for reading to students, but I do feel it is important to come to some specific understanding of why oral interpretation is a necessary tool for the English teacher in a high school. It is apparent that K-5 teachers need to read to their students (especially those who now use the Nebraska materials), but it is not readily apparent that high school teachers need to read to their students "almost daily." It is assumed that high school students know how to read.

"*Why* read to high school students?" In order to answer that question, I want to discuss the possibility that high school students should be read to rather than do the reading. I want to consider briefly the purpose or purposes of teaching literature. With the objective of the literature program in mind, I then want to explore some of the reasons why oral interpretation can help effect the desired results. I will conclude by giving some specific uses of oral interpretation in high school English classes.

I feel, for the most part, that literature should not be used as a means to increase the oral reading skills of students (unless there is direct instruction in oral interpretation). Perhaps students should not read literature aloud until they have been taught to do so. Many high school students (this is based on my limited personal experience) are not good readers. An ineffective reader—student or teacher—will probably obscure or miss the meaning, break the thought, and lose the feeling for himself and the rest of the class. Students often read without expression in a monotonous or singsong manner or else try too hard to put expression into their reading. This second group of "We Try Hard" often put the emphasis on the wrong syllable. In either case, they probably get but a modicum of the thought content and give very little of it to anyone else.

It will be the unusual student who has good basic reading skills, a complete understanding of the material, and the courage to express emotion in front of his peer group. Adolescents shy away from expressing emotion. Today's adolescents are often super-cool, sophisticated, and above it all.

When students read aloud, there are often surprising and sometimes disastrous results. The misreading I can't forget occurred when a boy reading the part of a soda fountain clerk addressed a sad customer with, "How now, melechanody dame?" I was entertained, but I'm afraid that he and the rest of the class were wondering what it was all about.

I suppose that few English teachers would argue against including literature in their classes, but I'm sure there would be disagreement when it came to deciding why it was there. The cases for literature would probably include teaching literary heritage, building character and teaching morals, humanizing the individual learning about others and ourselves, appreciating literature, and the one given the most lip service today (it seems to me), enjoying literature. I think I agree with C. C. Fries, who wrote in *The Teaching of Literature* in 1925 that teaching literature is primarily to give pupils literary experience. "Enjoyment is secondary to reliving the experience." Let me interject here that no matter what the purpose of literature is thought to be, as long as literature is part of the English curriculum, part of our job is to help students become able to discern by themselves the fullest meaning of what they are reading.

Full understanding of the material is basic to reliving the experience. It seems that skillful oral reading is a means to understanding and reliving the experience. Asking students to acquire knowledge of the author and his works, the conditions of the times, and his relationship to other writers often adds little in a positive way to the understanding and enjoyment of a work of literature. Such information is often fogged in students' minds anyway. I have had students who could tell me all about Edgar Allen Poe: "He was a drunken dope addict."

An English teacher is equipped with a special knowledge of literature. By using that knowledge and oral interpretation he can help students relive experience through literature. For example, he should be aware of an author's intent, and he could help reveal that intent through avoiding or establishing eye contact. This brings to mind the fact that the teacher usually is standing in front of the class, and his entire body can be used to transmit thought and feeling. His facial expressions, posture, and gestures will be a part of the communication. A student, sitting or standing, might be puzzled about the author's purpose, and a student who understands the author's purpose would have a difficult time communicating that purpose fully while sitting in the middle of a class.

In addition to being able to understand the poet's purpose and to communicate it through oral interpretation, an English teacher has other special knowledge which students often lack, and this lack of knowledge often interferes with reliving experience through literature because understanding itself is lost. When I asked teachers what they read to students, the most frequently given answer was poetry. Poetry was often read as a method to introduce a poem and/or to aid understanding of a poem. Since poetry was mentioned most by teachers, I will spend more time with that area of literature than with others.

I assume that most students read poetry silently the same way they read it aloud, in short, badly. A special knowledge of prosody is necessary for reading poetry intelligently. One of the main reasons poetry is read so poorly is that the reader does not recognize the rhythmic movement. Either the reading is nothing but rhythm and rhyme, or the rhythm is so violated that the reading is broken and unintelligible. An English teacher should be able to recognize the metrical stress in a poem and use it in harmony with sense stress and thought grouping to help students reach an understanding of the meaning. An English teacher who understands run-on lines in poetry and who will read them not as end-stopped lines and who will recognize a pause within a line and put it there will be a greater asset to students' reliving the experience than a teacher who has students memorize all there is to know about feet and meter and rhyme scheme. In other words, a high school teacher of English should know about poetry in order to read it in such a way that students will feel the experience of a poem. If a high school class is looking at the elements that make a poem, a skillful reading can contribute to an understanding of the effect of the poetic elements.

Grammatical relationships of the parts of a poem necessary for understanding are sometimes worked out through a knowledge of subject, verb, object, and modifiers. In poetry, students can not always discover *who* is doing the acting or *who* or *what* is being described because of inverted or otherwise complicated sentence structure. Meaning then is lost. Meaning is often muddled because the relationship between subordinate and independent clauses is not understood. An English teacher should be able to discover the grammatical relationships of a poem and be able to express those relationships so that students will also understand and experience.

A teacher who can recognize the type of poetry present will be alert to the problems of interpretation that are related to it. For example, to a high school student, a poem fourteen lines long may be no more than another poem that is hard to understand. The teacher, on the other hand, should recognize the type of sonnet and through knowledge of the structure of the poem reveal the development of the thought and meaning to students. A teacher recognizing a folk ballad should be able to communicate the simple story objectively. A teacher recognizing a literary ballad should be able to communicate the subjective factor that is often present.

Teachers may want to read to high school students for a practical reason such as presenting material that students do not have copies of or access to. I suppose some teachers read because they like to hear themselves talk, and it's an easy way to fill part of a class period. No teacher gave the preceding reasons, but I think they may come into play every now and again.

One teacher wrote, "I find it necessary to read passages aloud frequently, or students miss things such as tone and humor. For example, satire in the Prologue to *Canterbury Tales*, Swift's 'A Modest Proposal,' and Jane Austen's *Pride and Prejudice*, and exposition in *Hamlet*." Another teacher wrote, "I've observed classes where teachers 'read' to students without feeling, etc., and I've noticed, too, student reaction! Violent distaste for the material since the *teacher made it sound dull!* I use oral interpretation specifically with *Julius Casear*, reading of sample speeches, etc., in speech. In English I read some very short stories as examples of particular types."

Lawrence Mouat says in *Reading Literature Aloud* (New York: Oxford University Press, 1962): "He who has learned to read silently can free the living word from the printed page and enjoy what he finds there." Since high school English teachers so often face students who have not learned to free the printed word, the teacher, while trying to teach that skill, can through oral interpretation (to quote another teacher) "make children 'feel' the story or poem as if they, too, are experiencing the events."

Uses of Oral Interpretation in Directing and Motivating the Outside Reading of High School Students • Dorothy Matthews

In this paper I shall consider the special uses of oral interpretation for a high school English teacher in motivating students to do outside reading and in devising methods for culminating this outside reading in interesting oral activities.

I agree with those who believe that stimulating an interest in books is one of the most vital responsibilities of the teacher of English and also the one most frequently neglected. I wonder how many high school graduates can honestly say that their English classes instilled in them a lifelong love of reading. I even wonder if those of us who train teachers impress them enough with the importance of this task or if we give our trainees enough techniques, especially oral ones, for getting youngsters "hooked on books." For after all, of what use are long hours spent in symbol hunting, metaphor spotting, and endless question-and-answer periods in literature classes if students become so alienated against books that, after graduation, they will never voluntarily read another poem or tackle another classic! And, unfortunately, too many English teachers are more concerned with "covering" their textbook and drilling on facts than with leading young people to find real pleasure through books.

Leaders in English education have long bewailed the "lockstep barrier," as James Squire described this system of running all students through one anthology after another in time-honored regimental fashion. The most encouraging breakthrough, according to Dr. Squire, is the definite trend toward more and more individualized reading in our nation's classrooms. It is my hope that this extensive independent reading be combined with, but not substituted for, in-class intensive work on a core of books selected to represent our literary heritage.

What are some of the advantages of such a complementary program of independent reading? First, it can obviously accommodate individual differences so that every student can read a book with value for him personally. With our classes exhibiting such a wide diversity of abilities and such tremendous differences in background, this advantage alone would justify the program. Second, and really overlapping with the first point, is the fact that independent reading can allow each individual to start where he is, in terms of interests and reading level. Third, this approach can permit the student to read at a different pace and with different purposes from those which are usual for his in-class work, which so often must stress slow, close analytical reading. Fourth, independent reading can utilize current materials and also give a balance of kinds. Fifth, it is more likely that a teacher can arouse an interest in reading when the student is given some choice both in book selection and culminating assignment.

These ideas, of course, are not new, and although their transformation into actual practices in the classroom has been somewhat slow, there are encouraging signs well known to anyone reading the publications of the National Council of Teachers of English. More and more teachers are allowing released class time for browsing, for in-class reading, and for small-group discussions organized around books. Many schools are setting up cheerful and comfortable places where adolescents can go to read—ranging from corners in the classroom to separate carpeted rooms with easy chairs and tables around which the young people can sit to discuss their reading. More school newspapers are carrying library news, and many teachers are following Mr. Fader's suggestion in *Hooked on Books* by displaying paperbacks in every possible place in the building and even offering them for sale in cafeterias and corridors. In short, there is a growing and noticeable trend toward getting books and students together.

But just bringing them together is not enough, for haven't teachers for years been asking students to read books outside of class and turn in reports? One of the chief difficulties, of course, is with the conventional idea of book lists and book reports. I make a practice of asking English education students at the University of Illinois if they really enjoyed reading when they were of high school age. Their answer is always a unanimous yes. I suppose this goes without saying since they ended up as English majors. But when they are asked if they enjoyed making book reports, the response is overwhelmingly negative. In the ensuing discussion in which we try to account for their reading pleasure's having been entirely divorced from outside reading assignments, they complain that they usually had to choose from books that were old standards when their grandparents went to school—the lists consisted almost entirely of novels by such nineteenth century figures as George Eliot, W. M. Thackeray, and Sir Walter Scott, with modern authors sparsely represented, if at all. Even those who enjoyed Victorian novels (and they would make up only a small percentage of an average high school class) point out that they detested the way they had to report on books—usually by "writing up" each one according to a set format, answering such questions as: "Did you like the story? Why? Who was your favorite character? Why?" Or perhaps they were asked merely to summarize the plot or list the characters with descriptive tags after each one. All in all, the students questioned tend to think the lists provided in their high schools were out of date, puritanical, and dull, and the reports, Mickey Mouse assignments which invited abuse. Their teachers used either what Steve Dunning calls the FBI approach, in which the teacher's object is to catch up with bluffers, or the account-keeping approach, in which the number of books read is made to seem much more important than the quality of enjoyment or involvement with any one.

I feel that the best means of bringing about effective handling of independent reading in high schools is to train English teachers with this specific job in mind. Let's consider what a teacher needs to know in order to direct a sound program of wide reading. First, he must know his students—this knowledge he can gain through questionnaires and conferences. Second, he must know the books with special appeal for adolescents. Ideally, he should take an English course directly focused upon such books, but at the very least, the trainee should be aware of the many bibliographies and book selection aids, especially those distributed by the National Council of Teachers of English and the American Library Association. Third, a teacher must learn to be an opportunist with a real sense of timing so that he can take advantage of every chance to introduce the right book at the right time (more about this later). And finally, he must know how to devise a wide variety of activities so that his students find reading a pleasure and not a chore. And it is, of course, the development of this last ability which we are primarily interested in at this conference, for successful use of many of the best techniques for motivation depends upon speech skills.

Undoubtedly, a teacher's most useful oral skill for awakening interest in books would be the ability to read aloud with effectiveness. Applications in the classroom are many and will be elaborated upon later. But, in general, a teacher may read to the class an entire work, such as a poem, fable, or short story; he may read a book up to a point of high interest and then stop, hoping his listeners will want to finish it for themselves; or he may read short excerpts, a practice with countless possibilities but especially useful for enlivening book talks and book reviews.

Perhaps, before going on, I should clarify the distinctions I make between these two. A book talk's primary purpose is to create an interest in a particular work and thereby to attract a prospective reader. It is extremely short and informal, only long enough to whet the appetite. A few background details, if vital, may be presented, and the general nature of the book may be described, but the talk should chiefly be a glimpse into the work itself; and one of the best ways to provide this would be through reading aloud from an especially good scene or passage, a device analogous to the movie industry's showing of previews of coming attractions. As with previews, book talks should merely provide enticement. A teacher who is really concerned with making readers of his students could find opportunities throughout the term for working in this brief kind of sales pitch. Also he could occasionally break the class routine by bringing in an armful of books and giving a taste of each through the reading of well-selected excerpts. Asking students to give their own book talks later in the year, modelling them on the teacher's example, would provide a culmination assignment of interest and worth both to performer and class. Librarians were the first to promote book talks as a sure-fire method not only for arousing interest in a specific book but for focusing wide attention on reading in general.

The book review, on the other hand, is probably less valuable for the English teacher as a motivation tool or an assignment possibility. The term "review" naturally implies coverage, and the better the coverage, the less likely it is that students hearing the review will feel it necessary to read the book for themselves. Therefore, a teacher would find little occasion for the familiar "table-of-contents" type of the women's club variety, in which a book is fully described from start to finish with evaluative concluding remarks. But there are other kinds with real classroom potential. For instance, the "comparative" type review, in which a recent book is seen as it contrasts or compares with another, could well be used to tie in-class work with outside reading possibilities. What is known as the "attitude" book review could also be relevant in many teaching situations. This is the type in which the reviewer is chiefly concerned with expressing an idea or viewpoint and thus reads from a book primarily for illustration.

Skill at storytelling is another aspect of oral interpretation which would be invaluable for the English teacher. Unfortunately, it is an art which tends to be overlooked in training for the secondary level. A recent survey showed that almost all storytelling instruction occurs in courses required of elementary school teachers only. Proficiency in this art can be just as valuable in working with adolescents. Through it a teacher can aquaint his pupils with such materials as folk tales, ghost stories, and legends, all of which are part of the oral tradition. In fact, to be properly appreciated, such narratives must be heard, and then their appeal is natural and sure. Evidence that adolescents react with enthusiasm to storytelling can be found in the Cleveland area, where regular programs based on hero cycles have attracted wide audiences of teenagers.

Other useful skills are those involving group activities. A teacher experienced in choral reading, chamber theatre, and readers theatre can devise exciting plans for assignments to culminate independent reading projects. These group-prepared programs can, in turn, serve to suggest to the rest of the class possible new directions for future reading.

The successful handling of discussion is another art which requires study and practice. Any veteran teacher, I'm sure, would testify to its vital importance in the English classroom, especially in organizing and administering group work. It takes considerable skill to be able to conduct successfully the simultaneous operation of a number of group discussions. But since training for this, along with that for directing dramatic improvisations, would be provided in courses other than those in oral interpretation, I will merely mention in passing my conviction that they should be given more prominence in the total picture of the preparation of teachers of English.

Now I'd like to point out some specific examples of how and with what materials a teacher might apply these skills in actual classroom practice. I am organizing my suggestions around what I consider to be the basic principle involved in motivating and directing outside reading: Begin with student interests and then (1) deepen, (2) broaden, and, finally, (3) create new interests.

The most logical place to begin in planning individualized reading is with already existing student interests. The teacher's first job then is to deepen these interests through suggesting more books on the same subject or of the same type. No doubt this is the path of least resistance. The ideal procedure would be for the teacher to hold private and regular conferences with each student in order to talk about his reading, but since few schools can afford this kind of program, which by its very nature practically necessitates either very small classes or some kind of team teaching, the next best thing is to divide a class into groups based upon some common interest, as revealed in questionnaire replies. For instance, a teacher might form a group of those girls who listed among their favorite books *The Secret Garden* and the Nancy Drew mysteries. Knowing this about their tastes, the teacher could suggest some sure-fire but more mature and better written books with the same kind of appeal, such as the perennially popular *Rebecca* by Daphne du Maurier or one of Mary Stewart's more recent thrillers. In time, it would be hoped, he could direct the girls to a choice of books with real literary value. Works with the same ingredients of suspense, such as Charlotte Brontë's *Jane Eyre* or Henry James' *The Turn of the Screw*, would be possible follow-ups. In this way, the students have been given the opportunity, at least, to proceed up the ladder of literary awareness. It certainly helps in directing the reading of small groups if the teacher has received training in the giving of book talks.

Another way of grouping students might be on the basis of a common interest in a theme or a specialized subject. For example, boys interested in science but bored by English could be encouraged to read the authentically conceived science fiction of Isaac Asimov or Robert Heinlein. They might be enticed through book talks into trying biographies, essays, and even poetry, if they hear some samples from such a collection as *Imagination's Other Place*, which was anthologized by Helen Plotz especially for readers with interest in science and mathematics. These boys would probably find it stimulating to be assigned to plan together a program centered, say, on scientific achievements rather than to write book reports. And a teacher who is familiar with readers theatre would have a lot of ideas to suggest for selecting materials, organizing, and planning for such programs.

There is more of a problem when reluctant students reply on their questionnaires that they have neither favorite books nor special interests, but a teacher can capitalize even upon their common recalcitrance and lack of rapport with adults by grouping them together. Role playing would be a good motivating device for these nonreaders since it would involve them all in an activity which not only is within their range of capability but also actually provides an outlet for frustration. For instance, they might be asked to imagine their reaction to being told, while in the midst of preparation for a night out with their friends, that they must break all plans to be at the bedside of a dying grandparent. Student role playing of this incident might be followed by the teacher's reading from the scene depicting the situation similar to this in Jessamyn West's *Cress Delahanty*. Or improvisation of the role of a boy explaining an exam failure could precede the teacher's oral interpretation of the painful farewell between Holden Caulfield and his puzzled teacher, Mr. Spenser, in *The Catcher in the Rye*. Even the most negative student would enjoy this comic view of the world as seen through the eyes of a fellow sufferer and might be tempted to read the entire work on his own.

The foregoing are just a few examples of the use of oral interpretation in activities which may motivate reading within a common interest group. Other ideas are easily found in professional journals.

A teacher has not only individual interests with which to start but also concerns shared by the entire age group. These interests can then be broadened with the help of oral techniques. What are teenagers typically interested in? The answer certainly must include music, movies, television, and careers. And what adolescent is not interested in members of his own age group? A wise teacher may use any of these as natural starting points for reading motivation.

Let's look at ways in which a teacher might capitalize upon the adolescent's interest in music and the latest recordings. He could call class attention to the words of such popular songs as Simon and Garfunkel's "Sounds of Silence," "I Am a Rock," and "A Most Peculiar Man" by reading them aloud, and then he could set students in search of poems with the same themes of loneliness and alienation. A student-prepared program of records interspersed with readings would certainly reach students ordinarily unresponsive to poetry. Simon and Garfunkel's musical version of E. A. Robinson's "Richard Cory" would be a natural. Or an interest in the Beatles could be exploited by the teacher's oral reading of selections from John Lennon's delightfully zany *In His Own Write*, which in turn could serve to broaden a class's interest to the nonsense of Ogden Nash and perhaps even to the nineteenth century masters—W. S. Gilbert, Edward Lear, and Lewis Carroll. That some link already exists can be heard in the lyrics to the Wonderland-inspired "White Rabbit" recorded by the Jefferson Airplane.

The typical teenager's interest in movie going can also be used as a springboard to books. For instance, when the film version of *In Cold Blood* was playing in town, I brought to my college class some clippings from the *Life* coverage of the Clutter murders and paperbacks of other works by Capote. Then I spent part of the period reading from these. I chose excerpts from the pathetic section from *In Cold Blood* in which Perry's childhood is described and then read, for contrast, from the same author's beautifully moving telescript, *A Christmas Memory*. Then I turned to passages from his strange first novel with the young-boy protagonist, *Other Voices, Other Rooms*, and from his equally bizarre short story, "Miriam," which I read from the reprint in *Mademoiselle*. I saw results the very next week when some students asked if they could have class time for a discussion of their readings in Capote and their reactions to the movie, which almost everyone had seen by then. Every month provides at least one, and sometimes many, possibilities for such timely readings from novels on which current movies are based. But it takes a teacher trained to read well aloud to capitalize upon such chances to broaden interests.

Television offers similar possibilities. A teacher alert to the teenage fascination, for instance, with the CBS-TV series *The Prisoner*, starring Patrick McGoohan, would have been aware that that popularity gave him an excellent entrée for introducing through oral reading Ayn Rand's *Anthem* or George Orwell's *1984*, novels with intriguing parallels. Or he could take advantage of teenage enthusiasm for the satire of the Smothers Brothers by reading samples of parodies of fairy tales, fables, and Shakespeare in the works of James Thurber and Richard Armour. The appeals are the same.

Another way a teacher can turn an interest in movies and television to his purposes is by checking in advance with TV studios to find the year's schedule for movie reruns and dramatic "specials." Then he can encourage his class to read, prior to the telecast, the works upon which they're based. This is especially useful for awakening an interest in play reading. He could either give the class previews by reading short scenes himself or have the students read the play aloud in groups, each one small enough so that every group member has a part. Young people too shy to read in front of an entire class lose their self-consciousness and read their lines with enthusiasm when there is no audience at all—only participants.

An interest in careers is another natural for adolescents and one that can be used by a teacher for suggesting new reading channels. Many high schools feature a Career Day. Why couldn't an English teacher take advantage of this by letting students themselves plan class for this occasion? They could be assigned to find a book centering on the vocation which most appeals to them, find a section in their books which best reveals the attraction of this kind of career, and then read it aloud to the class. For example, a girl hoping for a stage career might read from Agnes de Mille's *Dance to the Piper* or Moss Hart's *Act One*, or a boy set on becoming a doctor might like to choose from one of the Tom Dooley books.

Another typical teenage interest that can be exploited in order to broaden reading is the adolescent's natural curiosity about others his own age. One teacher I know reports being able to interest her high school classes in literature about other countries by introducing them to world tape correspondence. Students read books about the land of their tape pal, record selected passages, then ask questions to be answered by return tape. Others find books which best describe their own lives, read selections onto tape, and send it overseas for reactions. A teacher with oral interpretation training would be prepared to coach high school students as they work on their readings.

A real advantage of the above methods is that they create a demand for books other than novels. As J. N. Hook has pointed out, although nonfiction has for the last fifteen years been outselling fiction, high school book lists and almost all required outside reading are noticeably novel-centered. Students should be encouraged not only to deepen and broaden their interests but also to extend the range of types they select.

This can often be done best in what is called enrichment reading—that assigned in conjunction with in-class work. Here there are many opportunities for a teacher to suggest a variety of types through oral means. For instance, he might read aloud not only from historical novels but also from biographies and memoirs to add dimensions to assignments in a survey course. Or he could time his oral presentation of such ballads as "John Henry" or "Mike Fink" to coincide with study of the westward expansion. A good assignment for reluctant readers would be to collect other ballads which might fit in at various other points of in-class work.

In fact, it is in the area of enrichment reading that a teacher's ability to read aloud can be used to best advantage. Why not, for instance, read one of John Donne's powerful sermons while the class is studying his poetry? Many are short and would be enlightening since they reveal the same tensions so evident in the poet's dynamic verse. Or while assigning from *Canterbury Tales*, a teacher could read from Marchette Chute's *Geoffrey Chaucer of England*. A good section would be that describing the writer's home over the London gate, from which he could observe so many kinds of men. Or while studying *Beowulf*, a teacher could introduce the idea of analogues by telling the folk tale "The Bear's Son."

Outside reading groups could also be used to enrich a literature class. For instance, a teacher could ask five or six students to read the same book and then give them a date for reporting to the class in some original way. For example, *Robinson Crusoe* could be presented when the class is studying the literature of the Restoration and early eighteenth century. I have seen this book cleverly presented in a "To Tell the Truth" format. Each of three students excerpted passages from the book to describe the main character from a different vantage point—(1) Robinson as a bold and daring hero, a person to emulate; (2) Robinson as a very ordinary, home-loving man, forced reluctantly by circumstances into adventures; and (3) Robinson as a ne'er-do-well, motivated only by self-interest, a scoundrel not only unheroic but actually villainous in his readiness to exploit ruthlessly everyone he meets. After each of the three claimed to be Robinson Crusoe and read from his cutting for proof, the moderator asked for the real Robinson Crusoe to stand. Of course, all three rose to their feet. This kind of program demonstrated more effectively than lecture the many dimensions of Defoe's classic, and it was both challenging to prepare and fun to watch. I've seen *Pilgrim's Progress* effectively presented as chamber theatre, and I've heard an impressive choral reading from T. S. Eliot's *Murder in the Cathedral*. Another unusual program was a lecture recital telling the love story of the Brownings through a reading of letters and poetry.

The classroom situations I've been describing should give some idea of uses of oral interpretation to an English teacher in deepening and broadening the interests of students—individual interests, those shared with most adolescents, or interests arising from classroom work. A teacher who is watchful for any opportunity for providing reading motivation will concurrently be creating new interests as a natural concomitant. He could also attempt to open unexplored avenues by using up-to-date materials whenever possible instead of depending upon timeworn lists. I'm sure that many teachers returned from the NCTE Houston convention, which featured contemporary poets, with favorite poems to share. Often current events offer possibilities. For example, the class session following the murder of Martin Luther King, Jr., could well have been spent by a teacher's reading from some of King's rhythmical prose. This occasion would also have been an excellent time to bring to class for book talks not only works about King but others connected with the whole nonviolent movement, such as the popular biography by Jeanette Eaton, *Gandhi, Fighter without a Sword*. Such timely introductions to books can do much to lead students to read kinds of literature which they would not ordinarily choose.

To conclude, let me say that I believe that the possibilities of awakening an interest in books through oral activities are limited only by the teacher's boundaries of ingenuity and training. Certainly the principle of motivating and directing outside reading is easy to grasp. One simply starts where the student is and then works to deepen and broaden interests. He can also create new interests by exploiting every chance for stimulating orally an appetite for books.

Such a course as we're envisioning at this conference might well provide instruction for the presentation of book talks and book reviews as well as giving general pointers on reading aloud. Practice in the use of audio- and videotape would also be extremely beneficial. And finally, I hope that the material suggested for oral interpretation will be drawn from literature of all types, but definitely from literature with special appeal for the adolescent. In this way, our course outline might be the beginning for making real headway in the practical training of English teachers by giving them the groundwork for awakening in students a love of books and for providing them with a chance to become involved in the aesthetic experience of literature through oral activities.

Findings and Recommendations of the ISCPET Conference on Oral Interpretation • T. L. Fernandez

The participants in the ISCPET Oral Interpretation Conference concluded unanimously that special preparation in oral interpretation for secondary school teachers of English is both feasible and desirable. They agreed, however, that many institutions might find it economically or logistically difficult to provide special courses for the secondary school teacher of English. In such situations the prospective high school teacher should be encouraged to elect a general course in oral interpretation if at all possible. The participants further agreed that the Guidelines for a course of study in oral interpretation could be adapted to the needs of the student who might not be an English major.

Upon completing the five-day conference at Monmouth College, the participants endorsed comprehensive Guidelines for a course of study in oral interpretation specifically adapted to the student preparing to teach English in the secondary school. The conference recognized that circumstances might necessitate individual instructors' making adjustments in or adaptations to these Guidelines. The substance of the conference's recommended Guidelines is as follows:

Course Guidelines for Preparation in Oral Interpretation

PREFACE

The course in oral interpretation herein described is designed as an upper division course for prospective teachers of English. In addition to this curriculum plan, the committee makes two recommendations: there should be a maximum of twenty students per section of the course; independent study and cocurricular participation should be strongly encouraged. Moreover, the committee wishes to emphasize that their recommendations are not conceived as ultimate or all-inclusive. Individual teachers will undoubtedly wish to make adaptations or amendments. Further, the bibliography prepared by the conference participants should also be considered as suggestive. Individual teachers will have titles they will want to add.

Objectives

I. To recognize that a literary work is an act
   The literary work is an act in that it exists as a living presence conveying sounds, movements, ideas, and emotions: it is a *felt form*.
II. To become aware of the contribution of oral interpretation to literary study
   The student learns how the act of oral interpretation serves the act of literature.
III. To learn the techniques of oral interpretation in the classroom
   The student learns to use the techniques of literary analysis for oral interpretation and to make his voice and body an effective instrument for communicating his understanding of the literary work.
IV. To become familiar by practice and observation with modes of oral interpretation suitable for classroom use
   While emphasis is placed on practice in individual reading, the student becomes aware of the varied modes of oral interpretation, such as book talks, readers theatre, chamber theatre, and choral reading.
V. To develop standards for evaluating oral interpretation in the classroom
   The student learns to judge his own and others' effectiveness as measured by ability to make the act of interpretation serve the act of literature.

Content

I. The Oral Approach to Literature
   A. The student should understand the rationale for the oral approach to literature.
   B. Oral interpretation enhances comprehension and appreciation of literature.
   C. The oral approach to literature involves translation of the literary text into vocal and physical properties. This translation is dependent on complete comprehension of the

text and on the development of a responsive physical and vocal instrument.
II. Literary Analysis Leading to Oral Interpretation
   A. Oral performance should be preceded by thorough analysis of the literary text.
   B. Analysis of organization and style determines the character of vocal form (quality, pitch, rate, and force).
   C. Analysis of point of view or "speaking voice" in the literary work reveals attitude which indicates vocal tone and affects characterization.
   D. Imagery may lead to kinesthetic response which may lead to empathy with the literary act.
   E. Analysis of prosody, figures of sound, and patterns of scene, summary, and description establish vocal rhythm and pace.
   F. Awareness of the denotative and connotative value of words in a specific text affects vocal and physical tonality in performance.
   G. Making use of such cues as diction, attitudes, syntax, and selectivity of details, the reader projects tensiveness of the text through qualities of voice and body.
III. Vocal and Bodily Techniques for Oral Interpretation
   A. Techniques of voice and body are means to the end of oral interpretation of the literary work and not ends in themselves.
   B. In respect to production and management of voice, the concern is with breath control, projection, voice placement, resonance, articulation, variety, inflection, stress, and emphasis.
   C. In relation to control of body, the concern is with posture, controlled tension and relaxation, facial expression, gesture, and movement.
IV. Communication with the Audience
   A. The reader should be sensitive to the needs and interests of his audience.
   B. The reader should be aware that selection of materials and preparation of the audience for listening should be appropriate to the grade and ability levels of the listeners. For example, in an average class of ninth graders, stories such as H. S. Harrison's "Miss Hinch" or O. Henry's "The Ransom of Red Chief" might be appropriate choices, whereas John Steinbeck's "The Leader of the People" or Wilbur Daniel

74   ORAL INTERPRETATION

Steele's "Footfalls" might be more appropriate for an honors class.
V. Evaluation of Oral Performance
   A. Evaluation should be based upon the effectiveness of the total performance.
   B. The oral performance should be consistent with the internal evidence of the literature.
   C. The literary act should emerge as the principal object of the performance.
   D. The performance should be properly projected.
      1. It should be heard.
      2. It should be understood.
   E. The performance should have vitality.
      1. It should engage the listener.
      2. It should elicit a desired response.
VI. Modes of Performance
   A. Individual performance
      1. Solo reading
         The performance in which the single reader reads prose, poetry, or drama should receive primary emphasis.
      2. Book talk
         The reader stimulates listeners to read a specific book or play by a brief talk that includes reading an excerpt from the work.
      3. Book review
         The reader gives a critical synopsis and reads excerpts.
      4. Story telling
         The reader retells the story in the spirit of the original narrative.
      5. Lecture recital
         The reader combines around a central theme various materials, connecting them by commentary.
   B. Group performance
      1. Readers theatre
         Readers theatre is a group activity involving delineated characters with or without a narrator and with focus placed offstage.
      2. Chamber theatre
         Chamber theatre stages prose fiction without rewriting the text, keeping the narrative form and placing the scenes on stage.

3. Choral reading
   Choral reading is an ensemble activity using voices in unison or in antiphonal or solo arrangements.

METHODS

I. A minimum of five prepared readings should be required. At least one should be chosen from literature suitable for secondary school reading.

II. Prior to oral performance, a written analysis, paraphrase, or discussion may be required.

III. Written or oral critiques should be offered for each individual performance. These evaluations may be offered by the teacher, the audience, or the reader.

IV. In connection with a major oral performance a term paper may be assigned for the purpose of exploring a subject in depth.

V. While written examinations are recommended in evaluating the student's total accomplishment in the course, the emphasis should be placed on oral proficiency.

VI. The student should be introduced to a variety of literary genres, styles, and authors.

VII. Video- or audiotape recordings may be used for self-evaluation or instructional purposes. Professional recordings, for example, refine critical judgment and broaden the student's awareness of modes of oral interpretation.

VIII. It is strongly recommended that the following teaching aids and instruction materials should be made available:
   A. Videotape equipment
   B. Films
   C. Kinescopes
   D. Recordings
   E. Audiotape recorders

SELECTED BIBLIOGRAPHY

Bibliographic entries have been categorized into four major reference groups, with the category of a particular entry given in parentheses after the entry itself.

I. Literary Criticism and Analysis
II. Oral Interpretation
III. The Teaching of Literature in the Secondary School
   (Items in this category contain information about literature programs in contemporary high schools. They should be used to facilitate special assignments in the interpretation of high school literature.)

IV. Performance Materials
(While many oral interpretation texts contain materials for performance, there are numerous special guides to high school literature which can be consulted.)

Items of bibliography which may relate to more than one specific category are so identified. The bibliography appears in Appendix V of this book.

In initial planning for the ISCPET study on oral interpretation, the study director proposed that if course Guidelines were agreed upon during the summer conference, the Guidelines should be tested in the academic year 1968-69. Inasmuch as the course in oral interpretation has been taught traditionally in the department of speech, the speech participants in the conference were asked to help in testing the Guidelines.

When the conference was concluded and the Guidelines for a course approved, it became apparent that establishing field tests of the Guidelines would prove difficult. Individual conference participants encountered a variety of administrative problems in attempting to get a pilot course established on short notice. By the time the conference was concluded, the several participants recognized that their institutions had already fixed schedules of academic courses for the ensuing year. Teaching assignments had been made. Moreover, it became apparent that in some institutions it would be necessary to receive special approval to teach an experimental course not already in the approved curriculum. As a consequence of these factors, it was not possible to find ideal conditions for field testing the Guidelines.

In an attempt to determine some responses to the Guidelines, however, several steps were taken. At the University of Missouri, the University of Alabama, and Monmouth College, the Guidelines were adapted to the regularly scheduled course in oral interpretation which included both English and non-English majors.

Professor ALLEN BALES of the University of Alabama reported:

> Since our fundamentals class [Oral Interpretation] is required of all speech majors as well as English majors in Secondary Education, it is not possible to follow the syllabus [Guidelines] exactly as it would be if just English majors were in the class. I have therefore had to tailor the use to these particular classes. Naturally, some of the assignments or units were ommitted. . . . I think that this would be the case even in small classes of English majors only. I am not at all sure but what there is too much to get into a semester course.
>
> The student reaction is very favorable, generally. The bibliography is quite useful. The future English teachers have stated that they believe the course will be invaluable to them in teaching. . . .

Professor FRANCES McCURDY, University of Missouri, reported somewhat similarly:

> Since classes could not be limited to prospective teachers of English, but continued to serve diversified groups of students . . . the Guidelines developed at Monmouth were modified.
>
> I believe students understood theoretically the first objective: to recognize the work of literature as a form of conveying sounds, movements, ideas, and emotions. Recognition of the theory, however, brought improved reading only when other factors such as intelligence, imagination, improved vocal instrument, and practice were involved.
>
> The students did recognize through their presentation in the classroom that oral interpretation made a contribution to literary study. It contributed in several ways. They read widely to find the "right" selection for their assignments. They recognized that the sounds made the literature more interesting and vivid. They enjoyed trying to embody the tones within a particular piece.

Dr. McCurdy further reported that video and audio recorders were used to help students become aware of vocal and body skills. Moreover, she found that students had less interest in listening to poems or records than in doing their own reading aloud. Professional recordings were used on a limited basis: sections of one or more recordings were used to illustrate such matters as phrasing and emphasis.

With respect to course content, Dr. McCurdy reported:

> Students experimented with group reading and several forms of individual oral reading. Book talks and choral reading were not introduced. Group reading was enjoyed but it took more time than was practical for class. . . . The final objective of learning to judge his own and others' effectiveness in making interpretation serve the act of literature was learned to a considerable degree by most students.

Dr. ELIZABETH WORRELL engaged in a series of discussions with faculty, students, and teaching supervisors at Northeast Missouri State College. These discussions were designed to consider the desirability of the proposed course in oral interpretation for prospective teachers of English. In response to a request for written responses, Dr. Worrell received such statements as the following:

LOREN V. GRISSOM, Director of Student Teaching and Professor of English Education, Northeast Missouri State College, Kirksville:

> One of my earliest impressions had to do with the uniqueness of every student teacher's needs and competencies. However, after two years or so, I became convinced that some factor other than intelligence and general background was influencing the classroom performance of certain student teachers in English. To be sure, the difference was especially noticeable in the literary area, but it also affected performance in other types of lesson. In countless confer-

ences with student teachers, I probed this matter and finally isolated enrollment in oral interpretation as the apparent cause of the important difference described above.

More specifically, the student teachers who had experienced one or more courses in oral interpretation were more dynamic and more effective in communicating with their students, both verbally and nonverbally.... These teachers were clearly more successful in making their students' experience with literature colorful, dramatic, and meaningful.

TERRENCE L. MOSER, Associate Professor of English, Northeast Missouri State College:

Inherent in all literature is the voice, or voices, of the persona telling the story.... The most successful way to demonstrate the various inflections of the voice is by allowing it to project itself through a reader as he interprets aloud. Most often when a student fails to understand a work it is because he fails to "hear" the voice of the persona properly. But when he hears the work read aloud, his problem is usually solved, especially if the reader knows how to read, how to interpret orally.... In my opinion, oral interpretation of literature is not only valid for the English major, it is wholly necessary.

FRANCES WALSH, Assistant Professor of English (Children's Literature), Northeast Missouri State College:

Oral interpretation... provides the necessary continuity between the student's literature study and his professional practice. Its content provides a variety of challenging materials; its conduct offers each student opportunity to explore, to experiment, to select, to organize, and to experience in depth problems, techniques, and appreciation. These materials and experiences combine to give the student richer understanding of literature and of the spoken arts, as a source of pleasure to himself, and to the students he will teach.

At Monmouth College, the course Guidelines were used as written for a group of twenty-three students enrolled in Speech 221, Oral Interpretation. The class was composed of students with a variety of educational objectives, including a group of English majors preparing for teacher certification for secondary school. The relatively small enrollment and teaching staff of the college made the structuring of a special section for English majors logistically impossible.

The Guidelines proved very adaptable, however, for both English and non-English majors. Students studied and evaluated the objectives of the course as stated in the Guidelines prior to beginning formal classroom exercises. It was concluded that the objectives were sufficiently broad in scope that every student could identify a personal goal within the stipulated objectives. Initial lectures, reading, and classroom discussions were related to the topics "The *What* Interpretation of Literature?" and "The Oral Interpretation of

What?" These exercises related specifically to the first two units of the Guidelines—"The Oral Approach to Literature" and "Literary Analysis Leading to Oral Interpretation."

Particular attention was given to Unit IV of the Guidelines, which emphasizes the communicative aspect of the act of interpretation. Students were encouraged to select materials related to the needs and interests of particular audiences.

As part of the course experience, each student frequently served as critic for the performances of his fellow students. Critiques were offered in both oral and written form. When written critiques were offered, four or five students responded in order to give a representative sampling of responses. Students also worked in groups with videotapes in order to make improvements in the physical aspects of delivery. Recordings of professional readers and poets reading their own works were used to supplement the unit on vocal manipulation.

Each student prepared the minimum of five solo readings recommended in the Guidelines. These ranged in length from 5 to 15 minutes and employed both prose and poetry. The initial selections were cuttings prepared from serious essays. Subsequent readings were drawn from narrative prose, poetry, and the drama. The final reading was a lecture recital of 15-20 minutes. Students were permitted to choose a theme and incorporate the works of several authors and genres, or to focus upon a theme recurrent in the work of one writer. As a spinoff from this exercise, several of the students were asked to give public readings of these programs in conjunction with the celebration of National Library Week.

In addition to the solo readings, selected students developed book reviews. Moreover, the class was divided into groups which dealt with the use of oral interpretation in teaching the short story and choral reading as an exercise in learning poetry. The general enthusiasm of the class was high, particularly when dealing with the group exercises and the lecture recital.

The following statements represent responses of students to the course as they experienced it:

JUDITH SHAUMAN, Senior English Major:

> As part of our course work for the oral interpretation class, six students prepared a Readers Theatre program to present the short story "The Death of Red Peril" by Walter Edmonds. This form proved especially effective in vitalizing the story through vocal reinforcement and physical placement of the readers. Six parts were created by dividing the story among four speaking characters and by assigning two readers as narrators. Limited only by their own

ingenuity and the physical environment of the classroom, the students were allowed a considerable range of creativity. The presentation led to an active discussion of the story almost as exciting as the presentation itself.

In my opinion, the Readers Theatre form meets two basic needs in teaching literature. First, it provides a variety of approach needed to enhance English classes and thereby offsets the analytical assassination of literature. Second, it brings the students into direct contact with the literature. The student is subtly coerced into an intense scrutiny of the story because he must assimilate it before he can present it. The teacher can step from the center stage position and allow the students to enjoy the literature by participating in it.

RENEE YOUNG, Junior English Major:

As a teaching candidate and English major I should like to note that the course in oral interpretation is not required but was recommended as a beneficial elective to prospective teachers. In my opinion, the oral interpretation course offered experience and training which I feel is extremely important for the success of a secondary school English teacher.

The primary goal of the student reader was to elicit group participation, interest, and understanding. Reaction to and interaction with the oral readings produced and enhanced discussions, which I believe to be of great value in the learning experience. For example, four students were assigned to present book reviews. Two of the reviews were prepared as lectures on the content of the book, while the second two focused upon oral interpretations of passages from the book. The book reviews incorporating oral interpretation were more successful in eliciting positive responses from the classroom audience than those presented as lectures.

Mrs. JOAN MAGUIRE, in the process of completing elementary teaching requirements, commented that in the choral reading exercise, "no one need feel left out . . . even the shy individual can take part." Moreover, Mrs. Maguire pointed out that practicing as a group helps to create a "feeling of working together on something worthwhile and rewarding."

And a candid observation from a senior student:

Another aspect of the course that helps a prospective teacher is the confidence developed as the course goes on. Standing in front of the classroom to read a selection is much like standing in front of a group of students of one's own. They *know* if the teacher is not confident, and once that happens, it's practically all over.

SUSAN ELIZABETH PHILLIPS, Sophomore Speech Major:

For one exercise in oral interpretation class, I participated in a choral reading with nine other students. We were given a general objective but no specific instructions. Proceeding on our own, the group decided to work with two poems by Vachel Lindsay: "Potatoes' Dance" and "The Congo."

In working on these poems our group encountered several problems which provided additional learning experiences. First, we had to ascertain which lines were appropriate for male voices and which for female voices. In addition, we divided the poems into solo parts, parts for two or three voices, and parts for the entire group.

A second problem was in discovering how to blend voices together on cue and in rhythm. This exercise required that we learn to think as one unit rather than as individuals.

As an experiment, we fashioned very simple costumes to reinforce some of the images projected in our presentation of "Potatoes' Dance."

When the exercise was completed, the members of our group agreed that we had not only accomplished something with our reading, but also had discovered the benefits of using group reading to introduce students to poetry.

The evidence collected in connection with this study indicates conclusively that oral interpretation is a valuable instrument in the teaching of English. While the Guidelines for a course of study in oral interpretation designed specifically for secondary school teachers of English have not been extensively tested, it would appear that the Guidelines are theoretically sound and practical when employed. Moreover, the Guidelines have the virtue of flexibility in that they may be used partially or *in toto* with the expectation of satisfactory results.

Perhaps the most significant conclusion to be drawn from the conference is that teachers of English and teachers of speech have a common interest in the development of skills in oral interpretation. The Guidelines reflect the common interest and the value of pooling the attitudes, ideas, and experiences of the speech specialist and the English specialist to enhance the preparation of future teachers as well as the teaching of English.

Research and investigation into the use of oral interpretation as an instrument in the teaching of English should be continued. There is a particular need to discover what the behavioral aspects of this exercise are and how they function. Oral interpretation is obviously a participatory learning experience. Attempts must be made to determine more validly whether the student of literature does indeed discover literature more quickly, appreciate literature more intensely, and retain what he has learned more efficiently when he has participated as an oral reader in the act of literature.

A most pressing recommendation is that more students preparing to teach English be introduced to the oral approach and that ways be found to provide postgraduate instruction for those teachers who have not had formal instruction in oral interpretation and who have expressed a need for the ability to use this important technique.

Appendix I:
Illinois State-Wide Curriculum Study Center in the Preparation of Secondary School English Teachers (ISCPET)

Director: J. N. Hook
Associate Director: Paul H. Jacobs
Research Associate: Raymond D. Crisp

EXECUTIVE COMMITTEE

Raymond D. Crisp, University of Illinois (nonvoting member)
John S. Gerrietts, Loyola University, past member and Chairman
John M. Heissler, Illinois State University, past Chairman
J. N. Hook, University of Illinois
Paul H. Jacobs, University of Illinois
Alfred L. Papillon, DePaul University, Chairman
Justus R. Pearson, Illinois Wesleyan University, past member and Chairman
Roy K. Weshinskey, Southern Illinois University, past Chairman

COOPERATING INSTITUTIONS AND PARTICIPATING INSTITUTIONAL REPRESENTATIVES

Aurora College—Roy L. Crews and Ethel W. Tapper
Bradley University—W. F. Elwood and Paul Sawyer
DePaul University—Margaret M. Neville and Alfred L. Papillon
Greenville College—I. D. Baker and Donald Pennington
Illinois Institute of Technology—A. L. Davis and Henry C. Knepler
Illinois State University—Victor E. Gimmestad and John M. Heissler
Illinois Wesleyan University—Justus R. Pearson and Clifford Pfeltz
Knox College—Michael G. Crowell and Carl Eisemann
Loyola University—James Barry and Sister Mary Constantine
Monmouth College—Grace Boswell and Ben T. Shawver
North Central College—Richard M. Eastman and Erling Peterson
Northwestern University—Sidney Bergquist and Wallace Douglas
Olivet Nazarene College—Fordyce Bennett and Vernon T. Groves
Rockford College—William D. Baker and Ronald Podeschi
Roosevelt University—William Leppert and William Makely
Saint Xavier College—Thomas Deegan and George K. McGuire
Southern Illinois University—Ellen A. Frogner and Roy K. Weshinskey

University of Chicago—Janet A. Emig and Robert Parker
University of Illinois—J. N. Hook and Paul H. Jacobs
Western Illinois University—Alfred Lindsey, Jr., and Sherman Rush

ADVISORY COMMITTEE

Harry S. Broudy, University of Illinois
Dwight L. Burton, Florida State University
Robert Bush, Stanford University
W. Nelson Francis, Brown University
Nathaniel L. Gage, Stanford University
Alfred H. Grommon, Stanford University
William Riley Parker, Indiana University (deceased)
Robert C. Pooley, Department of Public Instruction, Wisconsin (retired)
Loren Reid, University of Missouri
William D. Sheldon, Syracuse University
James R. Squire, formerly of the University of Illinois; past Executive Secretary, National Council of Teachers of English

Appendix II:
Background of the ISCPET Conference

The subject of this report is the ISCPET Oral Interpretation Curriculum Study Conference conducted at Monmouth College, Monmouth, Illinois, from June 24 through June 28, 1968, and sponsored by the Illinois State-Wide Curriculum Study Center in the Preparation of Secondary School English Teachers. This meeting was called to consider the design of a course in oral interpretation primarily intended for those preparing to teach English in the secondary school.

A basis for this project was established in a study conducted in 1967 which assessed the role of oral interpretation in the teaching of English.* The basic questions which this study addressed were (1) whether practicing Illinois high school teachers of English believe the ability to read aloud well should be an objective of their professional preparation, (2) to what extent English teachers read aloud to their classes, (3) whether those English teachers trained in oral interpretation find such training to be an asset. In responding to the survey, secondary school teachers of English testified that oral interpretation is a teaching instrument used almost daily and that skill in oral interpretation, therefore, is indeed essential to their effective teaching. The sample group of teachers urged that the development of such skill be an objective of their professional preparation. The Oral Interpretation Curriculum Study Conference was conceived in response to these findings.

Planning for the conference began with consideration of the composition of the working delegation. It was assumed that there must be representatives from both speech and English and that the representatives should be college and university professors as well as secondary school teachers. Speech must be represented inasmuch as oral interpretation is traditionally taught in college and university speech departments. College and university English faculties must be represented because this group directs and supervises the preparation of secondary school English teachers. Consideration was also given to the size and nature of institutions from which delegates would be selected. Invitations to representatives of English were limited to Illinois, since the original survey sampled only Illinois teachers of

*Thomas L. Fernandez, "An Evaluation of Oral Interpretation as a Part of the Professional Preparation of Secondary School Teachers of English," USOE 5-10-029, ISCPET SS-11-26-67, ISCPET, University of Illinois, Urbana, Illinois, June 1967.

English. However, speech participants represented a broader geographic base with primary consideration given to specialization in oral interpretation and teacher preparation.

The conference ultimately was composed of the following persons:

> Dr. Wallace A. Bacon, Professor of Speech
> Northwestern University, Evanston, Illinois
>
> Dr. Allen Bales, Professor of Speech
> University of Alabama, Tuscaloosa, Alabama
>
> Mrs. Vernell G. Doyle, English Instructor
> Arlington Heights High School, Arlington Heights, Illinois
>
> Dr. Thomas L. Fernandez, Associate Professor of Speech
> Monmouth College, Monmouth, Illinois
>
> Mr. Willard J. Friederich, Professor of Speech
> Marietta College, Marietta, Ohio
>
> Mr. Clarence W. Hach, Supervisor of English
> Evanston Township High School, Evanston, Illinois
>
> Dr. Dorothy Matthews, Assistant Professor of English
> University of Illinois, Urbana, Illinois
>
> Dr. Frances L. McCurdy, Professor of Speech
> University of Missouri, Columbia, Missouri
>
> Dr. R. J. McNamara, Associate Professor of English
> Monmouth College, Monmouth, Illinois
>
> Dr. Margaret M. Neville, Chairman of English
> DePaul University, Chicago, Illinois
>
> Mrs. Evelyn Work, English Instructor
> Monmouth High School, Monmouth, Illinois
>
> Dr. Elizabeth Worrell, Professor of Speech
> Northeast Missouri State College, Kirksville, Missouri

After surveying the general topic of the conference, the participants concluded unanimously that while traditional courses were generally available, a course in oral interpretation oriented to those preparing to teach English at the secondary school level was feasible and desirable. For example, such a course could focus more directly upon the literature generally treated in the secondary school; it could focus upon the instructional use of oral interpretation in the classroom; and it could be used to take fuller advantage of the background in methods of literary analysis which upper division English majors could be expected to bring to the classroom.

Nine of the participants were asked to prepare position papers to be presented in the opening sessions of the conference. These papers were to serve as springboards for the deliberations of the conference. Each position paper was related to one of three major topics: objectives of preparation in oral interpretation, preparing secondary school teachers of English in oral interpretation, and uses of oral interpretation in teaching English. These position papers, a summary analysis of the oral interpretation survey, and the findings and recommendations of the conference committee are contained in this report.

T. L. F.

Appendix III:
Oral Interpretation in the Preparation of Secondary School Teachers of English—Report of the Study
T. L. Fernandez

In establishing criteria for professional competency, the Illinois State-Wide Curriculum Study Center in the Preparation of Secondary School English Teachers (ISCPET) emphasizes that the competent teacher of English not only should have good basic speech habits but also should have the ability to read aloud effectively.[1] The good teacher is characterized as having "an ability to read aloud well enough to convey most aspects of the interpretive art—meaning, mood, dominant emotions . . . and variety." The superior teacher is expected to manifest "touches of expertise and showmanship [of] the professional oral interpreter or actor."

The references to teacher skills in oral interpretation assume that students are often introduced to various forms of literature through oral presentation, and that the English teacher who is ill equipped to present material orally may stifle or delay understanding and appreciation of literary art. In an effort to gather additional evidence pertinent to the criteria for competent professional preparation, however, it was decided to solicit testimony from the practicing secondary teacher of English. In January 1967 a study was designed for this purpose.

The basic questions which this study attempted to answer were (1) whether practicing secondary school teachers of English in Illinois believe that the ability to read aloud well should be an objective of teacher preparation, (2) to what extent they read aloud to their classes, (3) whether those teachers trained in oral interpretation find such preparation to be an asset. Finally, the study attempted to compare the attitudes toward oral interpretation of secondary school English teachers with those of persons who teach English and speech at the college and university level.

A questionnaire was prepared to serve as the basic instrument of the study. This questionnaire is reproduced as Appendix IV. Sample survey items were submitted for evaluation to several secondary school English teachers, college English professors, and college speech professors. This pretest group checked each item for clarity and pertinence. Suggested changes or deletions were incorporated in the final form of the questionnaire which contained eleven items.

Four items of the questionnaire related to the connotations and denotations of the term *oral interpretation*. Answers to each of these items indicate that the term oral interpretation connotes neither undramatic reading aloud nor acting, but that it is most often associated with the ability to express moods and emotions, to clarify meaning, and perhaps in this way to intensify the experience of the literature. Each group identified oral interpretation as combining certain aspects of literary criticism and analysis with matters of voice and delivery.

In the spring of 1967, 500 questionnaires were distributed to secondary school teachers, with a return of 305. Two hundred were sent to college English professors with a return of 96, and 200 to college speech professors with a return of 130. The high school teachers to whom the questionnaires were sent were selected randomly from the *Directory Supplement of Illinois Secondary Teachers for 1967*. College and university speech professors were selected from the *Directory of the Speech Association of America*. Catalogs of the several colleges and universities in Illinois were the sources from which the names of the English professors were selected.

Respondents were instructed to answer each item on a continuum scaled 0 through 10.[2] For example:

1. Should training in oral interpretation be required as preparation for teaching English at the secondary level?

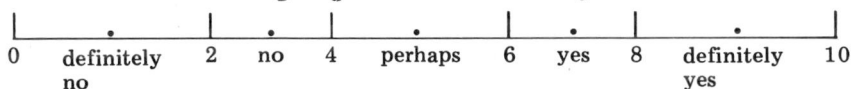

| 0 | definitely no | 2 | no | 4 | perhaps | 6 | yes | 8 | definitely yes | 10 |

2. In teaching English, the ability to read aloud well is:

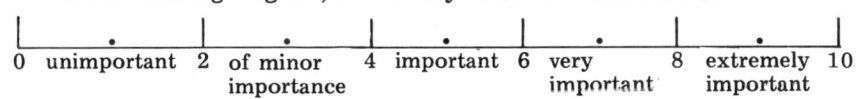

| 0 | unimportant | 2 | of minor importance | 4 | important | 6 | very important | 8 | extremely important | 10 |

3. As preparation for teaching English, my undergraduate work in oral interpretation has been:

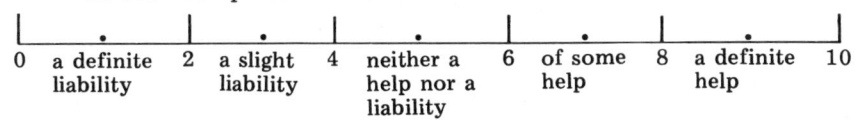

| 0 | a definite liability | 2 | a slight liability | 4 | neither a help nor a liability | 6 | of some help | 8 | a definite help | 10 |

Fifty-nine percent of the total sample responded to the survey. Secondary school teachers of English and college professors of speech were most responsive with 61 percent and 65 percent respectively. The promptness with which high school teachers responded may indicate a recognition of the importance of the subject matter. Five hundred questionnaires were posted on Monday, April 17, 1967, with a request for return within three weeks of the mailing date. Within three days, 200 completed questionnaires (40 percent) had been returned.

The initial item of the questionnaire sought information about the frequency with which secondary school teachers of English read aloud to their classes. High school teachers were asked to identify their practice, and college professors of English were asked to recommend an optimum practice. Continuum choices and ranges were as follows: never (0-2), once a month (2-4), at least once a week (4-6), almost every day (6-8), and every day (8-10). College professors of English indicated that teachers of English should read aloud to their classes almost every day with a mean response of 6.1. Concomitantly, secondary school teachers report themselves to be following this practice with a mean response of 6.3. It may be concluded, therefore, that oral reading is a recommended and frequently used technique in teaching English at the secondary level.

When asked to evaluate the importance of the ability to read aloud well in teaching English, the sample groups concurred in their appraisals. The mean response for English professors was 7.3, very important. Secondary school teachers averaged 8.0 and speech professors 8.3 on the continuum, extremely important.[3]

Reflecting these same attitudes, the mean response of each group to item c established that lack of skill in reading aloud is a handicap in teaching English. Respondents were given the choice of rating the lack of skill in reading aloud in teaching English as: definitely not a handicap (0-2), not a significant handicap (2-4), a possible handicap (4-6), a handicap (6-8), or a definite handicap (8-10). The means were 7.3 for English professors, 7.8 for secondary teachers, and 8.0 for speech professors. Responses to items b and c support the criteria identifying the professionally competent secondary school teacher of English as one who is skilled in reading aloud.

Item f sought to discover the amount of training in oral interpretation of the secondary teachers. The qualifying statement read, "As a part of my preparation for teaching English, I have had: no training (0-2), experience but no formal courses (2-4), one course (4-6), two courses (6-8), more than two courses (8-10)." The average teacher in the survey had one formal course in oral interpretation, but 117 (38 percent) reported no formal course preparation in oral interpretation. While formal course work in oral interpretation is not unusual, it is far from being a universal experience in the preparation of high school teachers.

Secondary school teachers with some formal preparation in oral interpretation were asked to characterize their preparation.[4] A mean response of 8.1 indicates that undergraduate preparation in oral interpretation was considered a definite help in teaching English. Those lacking preparation in oral interpretation, given the same choices, indicated this lack had been a handicap in their teaching.[5]

Finally, each group was asked to indicate their attitudes toward oral interpretation as preparation for prospective secondary school teachers of English. With an opportunity to choose from no formal training to more than two courses, each group endorsed at least one course in oral interpretation. The secondary teachers of English were particularly positive on this recommendation with a lower standard deviation, .9, than either of the other groups. The mean for secondary school teachers on this item was 6.0, and for speech professors 5.9, indicating there were many in both groups who would advocate two or more courses in oral interpretation.[6] Secondary teachers and speech professors were consistently similar in their responses.

Attached to the survey form was a blank page for those who wished to amplify their responses or offer additional comments. Of the 305 secondary school teachers responding, 127 (41.6 percent) included such comments. Three responses could be classified as negative. For example, one teacher wrote: "Forget about oral interpretation. Teach future teachers of English how to teach grammar." Sixteen (12.5 percent) made comments suggesting ways of improving the study. For example, one teacher suggested asking high school students about the importance of oral interpretation in teaching English.

The third group, 108 responses (85 percent) commented specifically on oral interpretation. The following comments are representative of those made by this group:

> It is virtually impossible to teach rhythm in poetry without oral interpretation. Mood is easier to teach when oral interpretation is used.... Audio aids are important, but these are second best.
>
> Despite what I now consider to be an adequate performance on my part, I still regret deeply not having had more formal training in this vital area, and I cannot recommend too strongly that English teachers should be better prepared for this phase of teaching.
>
> Students surfeited on TV will not listen long to a teacher who drones.
>
> Having had no formal training in oral interpretation, I sometimes feel slightly embarassed if I do not read a passage

smoothly or effectively. I think a course in oral interpretation would be beneficial.

Students like to be read to. They say material "comes alive" if I read.

Enthusiasm, understanding, and interest can all be engendered by the teacher's reading aloud. And once the youngsters get over the shock (many of mine indicate that reading aloud is for anyone under 7 only) they like it—it also builds up rapport beautifully. . . . I wish I were better at it.

In the final analysis, the survey revealed that oral interpretation is a subject of interest and concern to those who teach English at the high school level in Illinois and that it is an instrument used almost daily in teaching. Moreover, the secondary school teacher of English, as represented by the sample group, supports the hypothesis that developing skills in reading aloud should be an objective of programs designed to prepare prospective secondary school teachers of English.

Notes

1. J. N. Hook, "Qualifications of Secondary School Teachers of English: A Preliminary Statement," *College English*, 27 (November 1965), 166-169.
2. Continuum intervals were calibrated and means computed to the nearest tenth. A mean of 8.1 for example 1, therefore, would represent a response of "definitely yes" for the sample. Variance, standard deviations, and 95% confidence intervals were also computed. James McAllister, Associate Professor of Mathematics at Monmouth College, served as statistical consultant for this project.
3. See example 2.
4. See example 3.
5. The statement to be completed was "In teaching English my lack of preparation in oral interpretation has been: . . . ."
6. Item h. An undergraduate curriculum designed to prepare teachers of English should include: no training in oral interpretation (0-2), some training in oral interpretation (2-4), at least one course in oral interpretation (4-6), at least two courses in oral interpretation (6-8), and more than two courses in oral interpretation (8-10).

Appendix IV:
ISCPET Oral Interpretation Survey

Questionnaire Items

A. I read aloud to my classes:

0 never — 2 once a month — 4 at least once a week — 6 almost every day — 8 every day — 10

B. In teaching English, the ability to read aloud well is:

0 unimportant — 2 of minor importance — 4 important — 6 very important — 8 extremely important — 10

C. In teaching English, the lack of skill in reading aloud:

0 is definitely not a handicap — 2 is not a significant handicap — 4 may be a handicap — 6 is a handicap — 8 is a definite handicap — 10

D. Teachers of English who read aloud in the classroom should:

0 read as dramatically as possible — 2 seek only to clarify meaning — 4 seek only to identify the emotion appealed to — 6 seek to convey meaning and mood as well as dominant emotions — 8 seek to intensify the experience of the literature — 10

E. The formal study of literature based upon the oral approach is commonly called oral interpretation. To me, the term oral interpretation is most suggestive of:

0 acting — 2 reading aloud — 4 undramatic reading aloud — 6 reading aloud to clarify meaning — 8 reading aloud with controlled expression — 10

F. As part of my preparation for teaching English, I have had:

0 no training in oral interpretation — 2 experience but no formal courses in oral interpretation — 4 one course in oral interpretation — 6 two courses in oral interpretation — 8 more than two courses in oral interpretation — 10

94 ORAL INTERPRETATION

G. (answer part *one* or *two* as applicable)

1. As preparation for teaching English, my undergraduate work in oral interpretation has been:

0	2	4	6	8	10
a definite liability	a slight liability	neither a help nor a liability	of some help	a definite help	

2. In teaching English, my *lack* of preparation in oral interpretation has been:

0	2	4	6	8	10
a definite asset	of some help	neither a help nor a liability	a slight liability	a definite liability	

H. An undergraduate curriculum designed to prepare teachers of English should include:

0	2	4	6	8	10
no training in oral interpretation	some training in oral interpretation	at least one course in oral interpretation	at least two courses in oral interpretation	more than two courses in oral interpretation	

I. A course in oral interpretation should:

0	2	4	6	8	10
give minimum attention to literary criticism	give minimum attention to oral skills and delivery	emphasize oral skills and matters of delivery	give maximum attention to literary criticism	combine aspects of literary criticism, oral skills, and matters of delivery	

J. In evaluating the effectiveness of oral reading in the classroom, most attention should probably be given to:

0	2	4	6	8	10
the reader's voice	the reader's use of gesture and movement	the reader's selection and literary analysis	the reader's literary analysis and use of voice	the combined effects of selection, analysis, voice, and physical response	

Appendix V:
Bibliography

Bibliographic entries have been categorized into four major reference groups, with the category of a particular entry given in parentheses after the entry itself.

I. Literary Criticism and Analysis
II. Oral Interpretation
III. The Teaching of Literature in the Secondary School
(Items in this category contain information about literature programs in contemporary high schools. They should be used to facilitate special assignments in the interpretation of high school literature.)
IV. Performance Materials
(While many oral interpretation texts contain materials for performance, there are numerous special guides to high school literature which can be consulted.)

1. Aggertt, Otis J., and Elbert R. Bowen. *Communicative Reading.* 2nd edition. New York: The Macmillan Company, 1963. (II)
2. Aldridge, John W. *Critiques and Essays on Modern Fiction.* New York: The Ronald Press Company, 1952. (I)
3. Bacon, Wallace, and Robert Breen. *Literature as Experience.* New York: McGraw-Hill Book Company, 1959. (I, II)
4. Bacon, Wallace A. *The Art of Interpretation.* New York: Holt, Rinehart and Winston, Inc., 1966. (I, II, IV)
5. Beloof, Robert. *The Performing Voice in Literature.* Boston: Little, Brown and Company, 1966. (I, II, IV)
6. Blackmur, Richard P. *Language as Gesture: Essays in Poetry.* New York: Harcourt, Brace & World, Inc., 1935. (I)
7. Booth, Wayne C. *The Rhetoric of Fiction.* Chicago: University of Chicago Press, 1961. (I)
8. Brooks, Cleanth, and Robert Penn Warren. *Understanding Fiction.* 2nd edition. New York: Appleton-Century-Crofts, 1959. (I, IV)
9. Brooks, Cleanth, and Robert Penn Warren. *Understanding Poetry.* 3rd edition. New York: Harcourt, Brace & World, Inc., 1960. (I)
10. Brooks, Cleanth. *The Well Wrought Urn: Studies in the Structure of Poetry.* New York: Reynal and Hitchcock, 1947; Harcourt, Brace & World, Inc., paperback. (I)
11. Brooks, Keith, Eugene Bahn, and LaMont Okey. *The Communicative Act of Oral Interpretation.* Boston: Allyn and Bacon, Inc., 1967. (I, II, IV)
12. Brown, Stephen, and James Meredith. *The World of Imagery.* New York: Russell and Russell Publishers, 1966. (I)
13. Burton, Dwight L., and John S. Simmons. *Teaching English in Today's High School.* New York: Holt, Rinehart and Winston, Inc., 1965. (III)
14. Campbell, Paul N. *The Speaking and the Speakers of Literature.* Belmont, Calif.: Dickenson Publishing Company, Inc., 1967. (II)
15. Carlsen, G. Robert. *Books and the Teen-Age Reader.* New York: Bantam Books, Inc., 1967. Also distributed by NCTE. (IV)
16. Ciardi, John. *How Does a Poem Mean?* Boston: Houghton Mifflin Company, 1959. (I, IV)

ORAL INTERPRETATION

17. Coger, Leslie Irene, and Melvin R. White. *Readers Theatre Handbook.* Glenview, Ill.: Scott, Foresman and Company, 1967. (II, IV)
18. Commission on English. *Freedom and Discipline in English.* New York: College Entrance Examination Board, 1965. Also distributed by NCTE. (I)
19. Daiches, David. *Critical Approaches to Literature.* Englewood Cliffs, N. J.: Prentice-Hall, Inc., 1956. (I)
20. Edwards, Margaret. "Introducing Books to Young Readers," *American Library Association Bulletin*, 32, 685-690. (III)
21. Fernandez, Thomas L. "Oral Interpretation and Secondary Teachers of English," *The Speech Teacher*, XVII (January 1968), 30-33. (III)
22. Forster, E. M. *Aspects of the Novel.* New York: Harcourt, Brace & World, Inc., 1954. (I)
23. Frankenburg, Lloyd. *Invitation to Poetry.* New York: Doubleday and Company, Inc., 1956. (I)
24. Frye, Northrop. *The Educated Imagination.* Bloomington: Indiana University Press, 1963. (I, III)
25. Frye, Northrop. *The Well-Tempered Critic.* Bloomington: Indiana University Press, 1964. (I)
26. Geiger, Don. *The Sound, Sense and Performance of Literature.* Glenview, Ill.: Scott, Foresman and Company, 1963. (I, II)
27. Geiger, Don. *The Dramatic Impulse in Modern Poetics.* Baton Rouge: Louisiana State University Press, 1967. (I, II)
28. Gillespie, John T., and B. L. Lembo. *Juniorplots.* New York: R. R. Bowker Company, 1967. (III)
29. Grimes, Wilma, and Alethea Mattingly. *Interpretation: Writer, Reader, Audience.* San Francisco: Wadsworth Publishing Company, Inc., 1961. (II)
30. Grommon, Alfred, ed. "Preparation in Literature" and "Preparation in Speech," in *The Education of Teachers of English for American Schools and Colleges*, NCTE Curriculum Series Volume V. New York: Appleton-Century-Crofts, 1963. Also distributed by NCTE. (III)
31. Hemphill, George, ed. *Discussions of Poetry: Rhythm and Sound.* Boston: D. C. Heath & Company, 1961. (I)
32. Hook, J. N. *The Teaching of High School English.* 3rd edition. New York: The Ronald Press Company, 1965.
33. Langer, Susanne. *Feeling and Form.* New York: Charles Scribner's Sons, 1953. (I)
34. Lee, Charlotte. *Oral Interpretation.* 3rd edition. Boston: Houghton Mifflin Company, 1965. (I, II, IV)
35. *Literary Cavalcade.* A Monthly Scholastic Magazine of Contemporary Literature for Senior High School English Classes. 902 Sylvan Avenue, Englewood Cliffs, New Jersey. (IV)
36. Loban, Walter, Mildred Ryan, and James R. Squire. "Imaginative Thinking," "Literature: Basic Approaches," and "Literature: Drama and Poetry," in *Teaching Language and Literature.* New York: Harcourt, Brace & World, Inc., 1961. (III)
37. Miller, James E., Jr. "Literature in the Revitalized Curriculum," *Bulletin of the National Association of Secondary School Principals*, 51 (April 1967), 25-38. (III)

BIBLIOGRAPHY 97

38. O'Connor, William Van, ed. *Forms of Modern Fiction.* Bloomington: Indiana University Press, 1959. (I)
39. Parrish, W. Maxfield. *Reading Aloud.* 4th edition. New York: The Ronald Press Company, 1966. (II)
40. Pilgrim, Geneva Hanna, and Mariana K. McAllister. *Books, Young People, and Reading Guidance.* 2nd edition. New York: Harper and Row, Publishers, 1968. (IV)
41. Riols, Eileen. *The Place of the Book Talk.* New York Public Library Thesis, 1944. (III)
42. Rogers, Robert W., and Richard Wasson, eds. *Proceedings of the Allerton Park Conference on Research in the Teaching of English,* December 2-4, 1962. Urbana: University of Illinois, 1962. (III)
43. Rosenblatt, Louise. *Literature as Exploration.* 2nd edition. New York: Noble & Noble, Publishers, Inc., 1968. (III)
44. Sauer, Edwin H. "The High School Literature Program Reconsidered" and "The Teacher and the Art of Fiction" in *English in the Secondary School.* New York: Holt, Rinehart and Winston, Inc., 1961. (III)
45. Sloan, Thomas, *et al. The Oral Study of Literature.* New York: Random House, Inc., 1966. (II)
46. Sweetkind, Morris. *Teaching Poetry in High School.* New York: The Macmillan Company, 1964. (III)
47. Thompson, David W., and Virginia Fredericks. *Oral Interpretation of Fiction: A Dramatistic Approach.* 2nd edition. Minneapolis: Burgess Publishing Company, 1967. (II)
48. Wellek, René, and Austin Warren. *Theory of Literature.* 3rd edition. New York: Harcourt, Brace & World, Inc., 1956. (I)
49. Wheelwright, Philip. *Metaphor and Reality.* Bloomington: Indiana University Press, 1962. (I)
50. Whitman, Robert. *Play Reader's Handbook.* Indianapolis: The Bobbs-Merrill Company, Inc., 1966. (I)
51. Woolbert, C., and S. Nelson. *The Art of Interpretive Speech.* New York: Appleton-Century-Crofts, 1968. (I, II, IV)

FT. MYERS